MW00987795

Happy in the Lord

March 2003

Deacon Frank,

With much gratitude
and appreciation for your
kind support and guidance,
as we prepare for our
"Planning Retreat".

Kyriaki Thomas

Kyriaki Karidoyanes FitzGerald
Thomas FitzGerald

Happy in the Lord

The Beatitudes for Everyday

Perspectives from Orthodox Spirituality

HOLY CROSS ORTHODOX PRESS
Brookline, Massachusetts

© Copyright 2000 Holy Cross Orthodox Press
Published by Holy Cross Orthodox Press
50 Goddard Avenue
Brookline, MA 02445 USA

On the cover: Detail from St. George, Mosaic Icon, 1079. On the back
cover: Detail from St. Demetrios, Mosaic Icon, 1079. As found in The Holy
Xenophontos Monastery, *The Icons* (Mount Athos, Greece: 1999). Used
with permission.
The prayers found at the end of each chapter are from Orthodox liturgical
services as translated by the Monks of New Skete, Cambridge, NY.

Library of Congress Cataloging–in–Publication Data
FitGerald, Kyriaki Karidoyanes, date.
   Happy in the Lord: the Beatitudes for everyday: perspectives from
Orthodox spirituality/Kyriaki Karidoyanes FitzGerald,
Thomas FitzGerald.
      p.   cm.
      Includes bibliographical references.
      ISBN 1-885652-45-3
         1. Beatitudes. 2. Christian life–Orthodox authors. I. FitzGerald,
      Thomas E., date. II. Title.

   BT382 F59 2000
   241.5'3—dc21   00-040987

To our beloved parents

Michael and Tula Karidoyanes
Thomas and Jane FitzGerald

and our beloved spiritual fathers

His Eminence Metropolitan Maximos of Pittsburgh
Archimandrite Laurence of New Skete Monastery

As they continue to guide us in our "life in Christ"
through their love, intercession,
witness and direction

Contents

Preface

The following chapters are a series of reflections on the eight Beatitudes which are central to the teachings of Christ. The Beatitudes express the inner qualities of those who seek to follow Christ and abide by his teachings. From the earliest days of the Church, therefore, the Beatitudes have been used as a basis for instruction in Christian faith and life.

A number of persons have contributed to these reflections. This includes spiritual daughters and sons, family, friends, clergy, colleagues, parishioners, students, retreat participants, and those whom we have counseled. Some of these reflections were first offered a number of years ago at a retreat at the Holy Trinity Greek Orthodox Cathedral in Birmingham, Alabama at the invitation of the late Fr. Emmanuel Vasilakis. The reflections were further developed during our service at St. Nicholas Orthodox Church in Manchester, New Hampshire. The final draft of these reflections was prepared during our five years of service in Geneva, Switzerland.

While there are many who deserve to be mentioned here, we wish to express our most profound thanks and appreciation to Beatrice Bengtsson of Geneva, for her advice, encouragement and technical support as we were writing these reflections. We wish to thank Father John Maheras, Prof. Lewis Patsavos and Prof. Thomas Bird for the friendship and wise counsel they have freely extended to us over many years. And, we also wish to express our deepest thanks to our friend, Dr. Anton Vrame, Managing Editor of Holy Cross Orthodox Press, for his thoughtful oversight of the publication process.

Kyriaki and Thomas FitzGerald
Sunday of St. Thomas
May 7, 2000

Introduction

The Beatitudes

The four Gospels provide us with both a description of Jesus Christ's ministry and with a selection of his teachings. Jesus was engaged in a public ministry which lasted about three years. None of the evangelists sought to tell us everything which Jesus did or to record everything which he said during these years.

The description of the ministry of the Lord and the selection of his teachings are centered upon the great event of his death and Resurrection. As the promised Messiah, Jesus' passage from death to life was a sure sign that God was truly the victor over every force of evil, that he was more powerful than sin and death, that his love for us knew no limitation, and that his reign had been revealed in the midst of history. This was the "Good News" which each of the evangelists wanted to proclaim through their Gospels.

Writing from their own particular perspectives, Matthew, Mark, Luke and John have provided us with Gospels designed to proclaim the reality of Christ and to lead us closer to the Risen Lord. Christ is not a distant figure of history. He is the living Lord in our midst.

So, the Gospels were not meant to be a substitute for the direct experience of the Risen Lord. On the contrary, each of the evangelists has written his Gospel so that we might believe in the Risen Lord and grow closer to him. As Saint John says near the conclusion of his Gospel: "Now Jesus did many other signs in the presence of the disciples which are not written in this book; but these are written that you may believe that Jesus is the Christ, the Son of God, and that believing you may have life in his name" (John 20:30).

The teachings of the Lord as recorded in the four Gospels are but a summary of what the Lord said during his three years of public ministry. Yet, these collections of sayings are of the greatest importance because they provide us with some of the teachings of the Lord which were considered to be the most significant by the early Church. These teachings were the background for the preaching of the apostles and disciples. These teachings were also used in the earliest Christian instruction.

Saint Matthew has brought together much of the Lord's teachings on the topic of discipleship in chapters five through seven of his Gospel. This section begins with the description of Jesus going up a mountain. Surrounded by his disciples, he sits down and begins to teach the crowd which had gathered close to him. This collection of teachings is usually referred to as the "Sermon on the Mount." This "sermon" may, in fact, be a collection of a number of short discourses brought together by Matthew. In the description of the "Sermon on the Mount," the Lord seems to be depicted by the evangelist as the "new Moses" who preaches the Gospel of the Kingdom.

Beginning with the Beatitudes, the "Sermon on the Mount" contains many of the most important teachings of Jesus. These teachings especially emphasize the responsibilities of the disciple both to God and to others. These responsibilities characterize a new way of life for the follower of Christ. It is a way of life rooted in the fact that the power and reign of God are manifested in Christ. It is a way of life through which the disciple responds to the mighty act of God in Christ with thanksgiving. It is a way of life which sets the believer apart from those who have not received Christ as Lord. By following the teachings of the Lord, the believer bears witness to the centrality of Christ and the presence of the reign of God in this world.

The eight Beatitudes form at first glance a valuable introduction to the teachings of the Lord which follow, according to the account of Matthew. Some would claim that the Beatitudes express in a simple and brief way the fundamental teachings of Christ on discipleship.

Yet, as we look more closely, we should see that the Beatitudes first and foremost express the fundamental attitudes of the disciple as he or she stands before the Living God. These attitudes reflect the inner condition of the person who lives "in Christ." It is these attitudes, reflecting the presence of God's Kingdom, that are the basis for Christian witness and service in the society. When looked at carefully, the Beatitudes clearly affirm that our relationship with God is intimately bound up with our relationship with others within the reality of the rest of creation.

There are two complementary aspects of the Beatitudes. First, the Beatitudes should be viewed as words of congratulations offered by Christ to those whose lives are lived in harmony with the saving actions of God. Jesus is declaring that those who stand before God with love and who live in accordance with his Gospel are blessed. They are truly happy through their relationship with God. They are truly honored because of their relationship with God.

Second, the Beatitudes bear witness to the blessings which are experienced by the follower of the Lord. The faithful believer who stands before the living God with the attitudes of the Beatitudes will be blessed with the fruits of the Kingdom. The reign of God will manifest itself in the believer's life through comfort in the Spirit, through the inheritance of what is needed, through righteousness, through mercy, through the vision of God, and through being honored as the child of God. These are but some of the fruits to be experienced by those who share in the reign of God. These blessings of the Kingdom are experienced in the present. And, they will be fully realized in the age to come when the victory of the Lord shall be complete.

God desires that we be happy. He loves us and has created us to share in his goodness. True happiness, which is ineffable joy, is the fruit of our relationship with him. The Beatitudes celebrate this fact. And, they provide us with a direction which enables us to acquire the joy which the Lord offers us both in the present and in the life to come.

The Beatitudes have been used extensively in the formation of disciples through catechesis from the earliest days of the Church. Together with the "Our Father" and the "Creed," the Beatitudes have been the basis for countless homilies and sermons throughout the ages. We are most fortunate to have inherited the sermons on the Beatitudes from a number of outstanding Fathers of the Church. In the following chapters, we will incorporate in our reflections some of the observations from these great teachers of the Faith that were master interpreters of the Scriptures.

For the most part, the fathers of the Church have preferred to comment upon the Beatitudes as they are found in the Gospel of Matthew. We should note here that there are two versions of the Beatitudes found in the New Testament. The longer version is found in the Gospel of Matthew (5:2-12). And, the shorter version is found in the Gospel of Luke (6:20-26). There are some significant variations in the two versions. Because of this, students of the Scriptures have often discussed the relationship between the two versions as well as the differences in expressions and meaning. While there is no comprehensive explanation for these differences, we should not ignore the real possibility that our Lord may have taught the Beatitudes somewhat differently on different occasions. It is the version of the Beatitudes found in the Gospel of Matthew that we shall use in the following chapters.

The Beatitudes, of course, can only be fully appreciated in reference to the one who proclaims them. Jesus Christ, the incarnate Son of God, is the one who speaks these words to us. As we see in the Gospel, he is the one who comes to us as the embodiment of the Father's love for us. Christ is the one who reveals in his words and his deeds the reign of God. Obedient to the will of the Father, Christ has come into our midst for our sake and for our salvation. He is the one who is truly poor in spirit and meek. He is the one who hungers and thirsts for righteousness, the one who is merciful and pure in heart. He is the one who is the peacemaker and who is persecuted for the sake of righteousness. Jesus Christ not only proclaims the Beatitudes but also expresses them in his life. As we seek to live our life in a manner which expresses the Beatitudes, we shall be most certainly drawn closer to him. He is the Way who reveals himself to us as both Truth and Life (John 14:6).

From Our Christian Heritage

For everyone who listens to the Word of God should be disposed in his heart to order his life in accordance with what he hears. And neither should he think to praise the Word of God with his tongue while he ignores it in his life. For if it is sweet to you while you hear it, how much sweeter shall it be when you do it? For we are like those whose task is to sow the seed; and you are, as it were, the field of God. Do not let the seed be wasted. Let it bring forth a harvest.

Saint Augustine[1]

Prayer

O Good God, so very rich in patience and mercy, who are adorned and praised at all times and at every moment in heaven and on earth! You love the just and spare the sinner, inviting all to salvation with the promise of the good things to come! O Lord accept our prayer at this time, and direct our lives according to your commandments. Sanctify our souls and bodies. Set straight our reasoning. Purify and sober our understanding. Deliver us from every affliction, from every evil and illness. Surround us with your holy angels as with a rampart, that, guided and protected by their defense, we may reach unity in faith and the knowledge of your inaccessible glory. For blessed are you unto ages of ages. Amen.

Chapter One

Blessed Are the Poor in Spirit
For Theirs Is the Kingdom of Heaven

Before Jesus began his public ministry in Galilee, he went into the desert of Judea immediately following his baptism. The entrance of the Lord into the vast Judean desert was meant not to delay his ministry but rather to prepare for it with an intense period of prayer and fasting. For forty days and nights, the Lord lived in the desert alone. It was a time of intense preparation for the ministry which was before him.

This period was also a time of very serious challenge. The Gospels tell us that the Lord had three encounters with Satan. We now refer to these encounters as the "temptations" because in each of these Satan attempted to draw Jesus away from his mission and from his devotion to God the Father. Although the temptations are quite vivid in their imagery, the entire story is a description of a struggle *within* Jesus.

In the three temptations, Satan challenged Jesus to be disobedient to the will of the Father, to doubt the providence of the Father and to abandon the mission which the Father has given him (Matthew 4:1-11).

Jesus refused to yield to the prompting of the evil one. In his three responses to Satan's temptations, Jesus affirmed his obedience to the Father, he acknowledged the providence of the Father, and he professed his faithfulness to the mission he received from the Father. Although he was tempted, as we often are, the Lord did not sin by giving in to the deceptions of the evil one. Jesus rejected the ploys of Satan and remained steadfast in his faithfulness to the Father. The Lord affirmed his utter dependence on the Father and his desire to do the will of the One who sent him. Jesus remained centered upon God the Father and faithful to his will. Later in his ministry, he forcefully reminded his disciples of this fact when he said: "I came not to do my own will but the will of him who sent me" (John 6:38).

Poor in Spirit

Our Lord Jesus Christ says to us in the first Beatitude: "Blessed are the poor in spirit, for theirs is the Kingdom of heaven" (Matthew 5:3).

With these words, the Lord teaches that his disciples are persons who recognize their dependence upon God. To acknowledge that we are "poor in spirit" is to affirm that we are ultimately dependent upon God for our life and for all that makes our life possible. We are creatures who are fashioned mysteriously by the Creator of the universe. He has made us! We did not make ourselves! All that we are as unique persons and everything that we have in this world are ultimately rooted in the creative goodness of God. Our life and the conditions which make life possible are given to us freely by him.

To see ourselves as "poor in spirit" is fundamental to our Christian perspective on life. This attitude is not concerned in the first instance with the amount of money which we have in our wallets or how much food we have in our kitchen cabinet. A person can be blessed with many spiritual and material blessings and still live as one who is "poor in spirit." The poverty of spirit about which Jesus speaks in the first Beatitude refers first and foremost to our perception of our relationship to God. The person who is "poor is spirit" is the one who recognizes his or her ultimate dependence upon God.

It is not always easy to affirm that we are truly "poor in spirit" and to live our lives in accordance with this conviction. This is so for two important reasons.

First, we do not always want to recognize our radical dependence upon God. Deep in our hearts we sometimes rebel against this fact of reality.

We want to think of ourselves as being independent and self-sufficient. We frequently have the unhealthy tendency to see ourselves as "self made" men and women. And, we sometimes want to behave as if we are not related to God. Our own pride sometimes fools us into believing that our lives are not rooted in God and that our lives have not been affected both by God and by other persons.

Second, American society generally extols the tendencies toward rugged individualism and self-sufficiency. We are frequently led to believe that the "successful" person is the one who lives without regard for God or for other persons. The values reflected in so many aspects of contemporary society frequently denigrate a sense of personal dependence upon God and of interdependence with other persons. Genuine humility is not always a virtue which is encouraged and honored in our society.

Christians have a distinctive understanding of reality. It is an understanding which is based upon the coming of Christ and rooted in the teachings of Christ. As followers of the Lord, we believe that God and his saving activity not only precede our existence but also form the foundation of our existence. The power and sustaining goodness of God the Father, the Son and the Holy Spirit are at the very center of creation and of our own personal existence. We affirm that God the Father has created us. We profess that Jesus Christ, God the Son, has come into the world in order to unite humanity with divinity and, thereby, to restore us to fellowship with God. And, we acknowledge that God the Holy Spirit is now at work in our midst to conform each of us in a unique manner to the likeness of Christ. Christians believe that God exists and that God is the center of our existence.

The recognition of these facts is central to our Christian identity. We understand ourselves first and foremost to be human persons who have our origin and our fulfillment in the life of the Triune God. Each of us is created in the "image and likeness" of God (Genesis 1:26). This powerful biblical phrase means that we have an essential dignity which is given to us by God. We are created to live in fellowship with God. He calls us to know him, to love him, and to serve him within the context of our responsibilities and relationships in this world. So close is our association with him that we can declare that we are his daughters and sons because he is our Father (Matthew 6:9). God is the One who nurtures us with His goodness.

We have a natural tendency toward God which yearns to be fulfilled. We have an inherent inclination to know the One who has created us. In the very depths of our being, we have a natural desire to love the One who loves us. Deep within us, we have a natural willingness to serve the One who nurtures us with his goodness, even if we do not always feel this with our senses.

Saint Gregory of Narek expresses the intimate relationship between each of us and God when he says:

> There was a time when I did not exist,
> and you have created me.
> I did not ask you for favor,
> and you have fulfilled it.

> I had not come into light,
> and you have seen me.
> I had not yet appeared,
> and you have taken pity on me.
> I had not called upon you,
> and you have taken care of me.[1]

Affirming our dependence upon God does not diminish our dignity as a human person. On the contrary, our humanity becomes more and more realized as we affirm that we are rooted in God and as we grow closer to him. We are most fully human when we recognize that God is the center of our existence and that we are dependent upon him.

Healthy Dependence

Not every one who claims to be dependent upon God expresses an attitude which is appropriate and healthy. There are at least two types of "dependence" on God which can be seen in the lives of Christians. One type is unhealthy and can do great damage to our spiritual development. It reflects a poor understanding of both God and of self. The other type of dependence reflects an authentic understanding of God and our relationship to him. This type of dependence is healthy and it is absolutely necessary for the development of the Christian.

On the one hand, there are those of us who express the unhealthy type of dependence. In these situations, we often take little or no personal responsibility for our life or our relationship with others. We may claim to be people of faith who trust in the actions of God. However, upon closer investigation, some of us have a kind of "magical" belief that God treats us as marionettes and arbitrarily directs our life. We seem to believe that God will "somehow" take care of everything in his own good time. So, we believe that our responsibility is simply to wait for

God to act in our lives. For those of us who live this way, dependency upon God appears to be synonymous with resignation, inertia, and passivity.

Furthermore, we may even ignore our own sins and character defects waiting for God to do our share of the work. Or worse yet, some of us may even ignore the worsening malaise which occurs as a result of ignoring our personal sins and weaknesses while we claim to be serving God.

This unhealthy expression of dependence on God reflects an impoverished understanding of God. A person who expresses this type of dependency often views God as a stern and vengeful taskmaster who controls, or seeks to control, our every action. These persons may all too frequently believe that their moments of happiness are a direct result of God's arbitrary good pleasure and their difficulties are a direct result of God's arbitrary wrath. Rather than loving God as a Father, they actually fear God as a vengeful ruler. While this is not the understanding of God the Father which Jesus has revealed to us, it is an understanding of God many Christians have come to acquire.

Those of us who express this unhealthy type of dependence of God usually also have a poor understanding of the value of our self and others. Through our words and deeds, we diminish our own value as a son or daughter of God. We believe that we are not "good enough" to be a child of God. We also may fail to see other persons as children of the living God and to treat them accordingly. While we may profess our faith in God the Creator, we fail to remember that the human person is created in the "image and likeness of God" and is called to share in his goodness. We forget that the human person is truly meant to be an icon through which God is manifest in the present.

Regretfully, there are Christians whose behavior expresses

such an unhealthy attitude of dependence upon God. Such a misunderstanding hinders their spiritual development. And, unfortunately, their example of the Christian life is not usually one which is appealing to others who are seeking a clear under- standing of Christ and the message of his Gospel.

A certain number of these persons may have progressed down this path so far as to have come to believe that they are now the "experts" on Christian life and are entitled to judge others. The "fruits" of this include shaming and authoritarian relationships, paranoia and secrecy, delusions of grandeur, po- larization, division and schism. Let us remember, we are told by the Lord that "every good tree brings forth good fruit; but a corrupt tree brings forth evil fruit" (Mt. 8:17) and that "by their fruits you shall know them" (Mt. 8:20).

The appropriate understanding of our dependence upon God is expressed by those of us who affirm the understanding of God, self, and others which is truly rooted in the teachings of Christ.

Jesus teaches us that God is our loving Father (Matthew 6:9). Not only has he created each of us but also he cares about each of us in a distinctive and deeply personal way. While we are called to seek his will in all things, he does not arbitrarily control our lives. He does not even compel us to love him. Rather, he has blessed us with the freedom to choose to live as his sons and daughters. He has given us the opportunity to be his co-workers in this world. Even when we sin and turn away from him, he does not abandon us. Like a loving Father, he loves us and waits for our return.

The healthy understanding of dependence upon God means not only that we know him to be the source of life and holiness but also that we view ourselves as persons of value, created in his "image and likeness." Because of him, we have a dignity which can never be taken away. As his sons and daughters, we are gifted with an invitation freely and responsibility to join with God in bringing wholeness to our own lives and the lives of others. This understanding of genuine dependence means that we have a profound respect for our own self and for others. This is so because each of us is a unique person who is loved by God. Experiencing the love which God has for us, we treasure ourselves and others as his handiwork. We see ourselves and others as persons with the opportunity, if we so choose, to manifest the presence of God in this world.

This sense of healthy dependence upon God also provides us with a basis for the recognition of our human limitations. While we are called to be the servants of God in this world, we do not have the ability to control the lives of others. Simply put, we are not God. We cannot force others to change. We cannot force others to accept the Christian way of life. Although we can pray for their well-being and may provide them with generous assistance, guidance and a good example, we must recognize that all persons are free to believe as they wish and to behave in a manner which they deem to be appropriate.

Likewise, we must remember that there are many circumstances and events in life that are "out of our control." Times will come when we may be confronted by profoundly negative or difficult experiences. These may include evil circumstances, betrayal, loss, hardship, illness and other tragedies over which we often have little or no control. Despite our good intentions and our prayers, things happen in life which are beyond our ability to prevent. In moments such as these, we are confronted with our own limitations. And, at the same time, we are reminded of our need to affirm our ultimate dependence upon God. He does not abandon us in times of adversity. Yet, it is only through consciously affirming our utter, radical dependence upon him that we are able to experience his presence in the midst of difficult situations.

True humility, therefore, involves a recognition that each of us is dependent upon God and that each of us has limitations which must be acknowledged. The humble person is the one who stands honestly before God without pretense and false pride. Far from being an expression of fear and timidity, true humility is an expression of personal integrity, strength and courage which reflect the teachings of Christ.

The Gifts of God

The recognition of our "poverty in spirit" before God our Father is the necessary precondition for spiritual growth. We cannot grow closer to God and deepen our own identity as his friends and servants unless we first recognize that our life is wholly dependent upon him. We must be ready and willing to stand before God with a spirit of humility.

From the perspective of Christian spiritual growth, the attitude of the self-made and autonomous individual is the basis for a spiritual disease which can hinder and ultimately destroy the genuine development of Christian identity and discipleship. A positive sense of our dependence upon God grounds us in genuine reality and serves as the basis for spiritual development.

Those of us who acknowledge our "poverty in spirit" and who recognize our ultimate dependence upon God the Father also come to appreciate another important truth of the Christian life. We come to believe that our life and all the blessings of our life are gifts from God. These gifts may be of a spiritual or a material nature. Among the spiritual, are the gifts of "love, joy, peace, patience, kindness, goodness, faithfulness, gentleness and self-control" (Galatians 5:22). The gifts from God may also be material. We should not overlook the fact that food, clothing and shelter are blessings. Even the money which is needed to purchase these and other material things are properly seen by the Christian as a gift which ultimately comes from God.

God is active in our life in so many ways. The material and spiritual blessings which we enjoy are not simply the result of our own efforts. These blessings are gifts which God gives to us. The Apostle James expresses very well this perspective when he says: "Make no mistake about this, my dear brothers and sisters, it is all that is good, everything that is perfect, which is given us from above; it comes down from the Father of all light: with him there is no such thing as alteration, no shadow of a change. By his own choice, he made us his children by the message of the truth so that we should be a sort of first fruits of all that he had created" (James 1:17-18).

All the gifts which we enjoy in this life should make us more deeply conscious of our absolute dependence upon God who is our Creator and Sustainer. Each gift comes to us as a blessing which can inspire us to be more mindful of the Giver of the gift. Each gift can also be a sign which can direct us more closely toward the God who loves us as our Father.

Yes, the blessings which we receive should direct our attention to God. But, we know all too well that this is not always the case. Sometimes we take our gifts for granted. We receive the gift but fail to acknowledge the Giver of the gift. Sometimes, we become fascinated with the gift to such a degree that it directs our attention away from God. Indeed, we may make the gift more important in our lives than God himself.

Spiritual and material blessings are all gifts from God. However, we are often tempted to turn these gifts into idols. They can become substitutes – very poor substitutes – for God in our life. Instead of humbly praising God for the blessings which he has given to us, we turn the gift into an idol and bow down before it.

It is possible for men and women with material wealth to be "poor in spirit." Yet, it is very difficult. The Scriptures remind us that there were a number of faithful believers who were persons of material wealth. Among these were Abraham, Joseph and Job whose stories are told in the Old Testament. In the New Testament, we could note Zacchaeus the tax collector (Luke 19:2) and Joseph of Arimathea (Mark 15:43). God blessed these persons with many material possessions. However, these possessions did not become impediments to their salvation. These persons recognized their gifts to be blessings from God, and they were grateful to their benefactor.

Saint John Chrysostom especially praises the example of Abraham when he says:

> Abraham was rich but loved not his wealth. He did not lust after the house of one person or the wealth of another. Rather, he went out to look for the stranger or for some poor person so that he could care for the traveler. He covered not his ceilings with gold but he placed his tent near the oak tree and was content with the shade of its leaves. Yet, his dwelling place was so bright that angels were not ashamed to spend time with him. They sought not the splendor of an abode but the purity of soul. So let us, beloved, imitate Abraham and bestow our goods on the needy.[2]

Sadly, we do not always follow the example of Abraham! Our material possessions often make us feel self-sufficient. We easily can neglect the needs of others. Our quest for the many things of life can lead us away from God and his service.

Jesus knew this very well. This is precisely the reason that he warns us about the danger of wealth. He tells us that it is difficult for a rich person to enter the Kingdom of Heaven (Matthew 19:23). He warns us of this harsh reality not because the material blessings are evil in themselves. As the example of Abraham shows, they are not. On the contrary, the Lord warns us because we can misuse our blessings. As we have already said, these gifts can be made into idols which ultimately become merciless, tyrannical "gods" in themselves. The very nature of idols seek to turn our hearts and minds away from God. Ironically, our quest for the things of life, can lead us away from our very Source of Life.

"Poverty of spirit" is a characteristic of Christian life which does not lead us to false pride, to arrogance, delusion or to self-sufficiency. The recognition of "poverty in spirit" before God leads us to a sense of gratitude and thanksgiving for all the blessings which we have received. With the words of David the Psalmist, we should be able to raise our voices and joyously declare:

> Bless the Lord, O my soul.
> From the depth of my being,
> Bless his holy name.
> Bless the Lord, O my soul
> Forget not all his favors
> He is who pardons all your failings
> Who cures all your ills
> Who preserves your life from deadly peril.
> Who crowns you with tenderness and mercy
> Who fills your lifetime with goodness.
> Who restores your youth like the eagle's
> (Psalm 103 [102]:1-5)

Prayer, Fasting and Almsgiving

Three very important ways through which we can deepen our relationship with God are prayer, fasting and almsgiving. Prayer leads us from self-centeredness to God-centeredness. Fasting by abstaining from certain foods for a period of time aids us in avoiding an attitude of self-sufficiency. Fasting reminds us of the providence of God. Almsgiving is an expression of our obligation to be caring for those who are in need. At the same time, almsgiving aids us in avoiding a sense of self-absorption. Each of these disciplines, when exercised wisely and with humility, enable us to affirm and to deepen our sense of dependence upon God, and to affirm our identity as his sons and daughters.

Jesus was a person of prayer. He frequently prayed especially prior to important events in his ministry, We know that he prayed prior to his baptism, before selecting the Twelve Disciples, before his miracles, as well as before and after his death and resurrection. Indeed, these are but a few of the many instances when our Lord turned in prayer to God the Father. Prayer was a unifying thread which ran throughout the ministry of Jesus on this earth.

Although each of his prayers were distinctive, each clearly expressed the sense of closeness between Jesus and God his Father. Each prayer of the Lord was a natural and a loving expression of his dependence upon his Father. Through the prayers to his Father, Jesus affirmed and nurtured the bond of the love which existed between them. Prayer was a special and very valuable way through which the Lord maintained his relationship of love with his Father.

Prayer may be expressed in a number of particular ways. Through our prayers, we can express our loving adoration of God in words of praise. We can express words of thanksgiving to God for all his blessings. We can offer words of intercession to God for the needs of others and for our own needs. We can ask for the blessings of God which lead us toward salvation. And, we can express words of repentance and contrition before God for our sins.

Prayer, however, need not always be spoken or sung with words. Sometimes we pray with utter silence. Indeed, there are times when only silence will suffice. The very act of consciously standing before God in silence is an act of prayer. This is the essential meaning of the Greek biblical word for prayer which is *proseuche*. In our silence we, as human creations, surrender our limited will to God and open our depths to him. It is from this place, where we stand in unconditional trust and attention, that we listen and wait in the presence of our loving Creator. This is the God whom we have been taught to address with the same intimate name used by the Lord, Jesus: "Abba" or "Father" (Matthew 6:9). Here, in the mysterious depths and silence of our prayer, we open ourselves to greater Reality. Through the power of the Holy Spirit, the ever-present triune God, comes to us... even if we do not "feel" it.

There is a common presupposition underlying all Christian prayer regardless of its different manifestations. This presupposition is the conviction that every prayer is a human response to the presence of God, our loving Father. We can pray because we know that God is with us, that he has created us, and that we are of the greatest value to him. In so many ways, he touches our lives daily. And, our prayer is always a loving and trusting response to his presence. Through our prayers, we open ourselves up to his presence, we remember him, and we affirm that we wish to center our lives upon him.

While the Lord urges us to be persons of prayer, he also warns us about the danger of hypocritical prayer. When we pray, we are not meant to speak "empty phrases" thinking that "many words," even intelligent sounding words, will make God be attentive (Matthew 6:7).

Furthermore, we are not meant to make a public spectacle of ourselves when we pray. We are not meant to pray so that others will be impressed by our actions. To counter these false understandings of prayer, Jesus said to his disciples:

> And when you pray, you must not be like the hypocrites, for they love to stand and pray in the synagogues and at street corners that they may be seen by men. Truly, I say to you, they have received their reward. But when you pray, go into your room and shut the door and pray to your Father who is in secret; and your Father who sees in secret will reward you.
> (Matthew 6:5-6).

The second important discipline which can help us deepen our relationship with God is fasting. The Gospel tells us that our Lord fasted before he began his public ministry (Matthew 4:2). The fast of the Lord is reminiscent of the fast of Moses on Mount Sinai (Exodus 24:18) and the Prophet Elijah on Mount Horeb (1 Kings 19:8-12). In each of these examples from the Scriptures, it is clear that the fast was not meant to be an end in itself. Rather, the fast was a means of deepening the relationship with God the Father, the source of all, and of avoiding a sense of self-sufficiency.

There are two basic expressions of fasting which have been a part of Christian spiritual life. First, a fast may be understood as a total abstinence from foods, from beverage, and from unnecessary activity for a specific period of time. It is customary, for example, for many Christians to follow this type of fast in the morning prior to receiving Holy Communion. This fast is to serve as a preparation for the reception of Holy Communion. Similarly, on certain days of the year, such as Good Friday, it is also customary for many Christians to observe this type of fast throughout the day. A light meal may conclude the fast in the late afternoon or early evening. A fast such as this can be helpful in assisting us in observing the particular solemnity of the day.

The second expression of fasting is concerned with the type of food or activity which is avoided. Some Christians choose to abstain from certain types of food and beverage on certain days or during certain seasons of the Church year. There is an ancient tradition which calls upon Christians to abstain from meat and dairy products on Wednesdays and Fridays. Similarly, during the season of Lent, which is the forty-day period before Holy Week, many Christians abstain from meat and dairy products. This abstinence is also a means of remembering especially the passion of the Lord and of preparing to celebrate the feast of the Resurrection.

When Christians are in a period of fasting, either on a particular day or during a particular season, they usually also strive to avoid any unnecessary activities. Because of this tradition, some contemporary Christians have developed customs whereby they "abstain" from television, or movies, or social events during the fasting period. As with the fasting from food and beverage, this type of fast is designed to focus our attention better upon God and his will. Indeed, these types of fasts can be very powerful means which alter our daily routine and re-orient our lives toward the Lord.

The Fathers and Mothers of the Church have consistently warned Christians not to become fixated upon abstinence from food during times of fast and, thereby, neglect the basic Christian virtues. In this regard, Saint Basil the Great says:

> Do not limit the benefits of fasting merely to
> abstinence from food, for a true fast means re-
> fraining from evil. Loose every unjust bond, put
> away your resentment against your neighbor,
> and forgive his offenses. Do not let your fasting
> lead only to wrangling and strife. You do not
> eat meat, but you devour your brother. You ab-
> stain from wine, but not from insults. So all the
> labor of your fast is useless.[3]

Every form of fasting should assist us in deepening our relationship of love which we have with God and with others.
This is clear the message which Saint Basil wishes to convey. If
genuine love is not the principle fruit of the fast, then the fast –
even the most stringent – has no value. Fasting is meant to
strengthen our loving relationship with God and with all those
whom God loves.

As was the case with Saint Basil, many of the great teachers
of the early Church also saw fasting as a means of identification with the poor and needy. By abstaining from food, we are
meant to remember the blessings which God has bestowed upon
us. At the same time, we also have the opportunity remember
the needy and to provide them with a share of our blessings.
Time and again, the great teachers of the faith tell us that those
of us who have an abundance of material things have a profound responsibility to care for the needy.

While recognizing fasting to be a valuable spiritual discipline, there are some serious dangers which must be avoided.
The first danger is to view fasting as an end in itself. As we
have said, a fast is a means towards an end. It is a helpful discipline which can aid us in deepening our relationship with God
by reminding us of our dependence upon him and his mighty
deeds. Because fasting is seen as a means to this goal and not an

end in itself, persons who are ill, who have medical conditions, who suffer from an eating disorder, who take medication, or who are traveling have never been expected to follow a strict form of fast or abstinence. The very young and the elderly also have not been expected to follow strict rules for fasting. Clearly, fasting must always be done with a realistic appreciation of our physical condition and limitations. The fast is not meant to endanger our physical or emotional well being.

Jesus clearly opposed any type of hypocrisy and false spirituality especially with regard to fasting. The Lord not only fasted but also he gave his disciples some clear directions on the manner of fasting when he said:

> And when you fast, do not look dismal like the hypocrites, for they disfigure their faces that their fasting may be seen by men. Truly, I say to you, they have received their reward. But when you fast, anoint your head and wash your face, that your fasting may not be seen by men but by your Father who is in secret will reward you. (Matthew 6:16-18)

The third discipline which helps deepen our relationship with God by reminding us of our dependence upon him is almsgiving. This term is the traditional one which describes the Christian practice of giving freely to those who are need.

Our Lord was a person who not only freely gave to others in need – he offered his life for us – but also provided us with many examples of giving. On one occasion during his ministry a crowd of more than five thousand people had been listening to his preaching. As the day came to a close, the disciples pleaded with the Lord to dismiss the crowds so that they could go home to eat. Jesus, however, was concerned with the welfare of the people. He gathered together five loaves of bread and two fish which the Twelve had been keeping for themselves. With the blessing of the Lord, the meager amount of food was multiplied so that all people could eat. Truly, it was a sign that revealed the love and care of God for his people (Matthew 14:13-21).

Certainly, the power of the Lord as God, who had entered into the human history, was unique and far greater than any power which we possess. Yet, the example of his concern for the needy is a very moving and important one. He gives us an example which we can follow in our own ways. Jesus took what he and the disciples had, and he shared it with those who had nothing. The blessing was multiplied.

In his Sermon on the Mount, not only does Jesus provide us with guidance on prayer and fasting but also he gives us some direction on the characteristics of the person who gives alms to the needy. The Lord says:

> Thus, when you give alms, sound no trumpet before you as the hypocrites do in the synagogues and in the streets, that they may be praised by men. Truly, I say to you they have received their reward. But when you give alms, do not let your left hand know what your right hand is doing, so that your alms may be in secret and your Father who sees in secret will reward you. (Matthew 6:2-4)

When Christians give freely to those in need, we do so as an expression of love for those who are created in the "image and likeness" of God. Our love for others, especially for the less fortunate, is meant to reflect the love which God has for us. His love is always free and generous. And so, the love which we offer others must be one which seeks nothing in return. It likewise, must be given freely and generously; extended with profound respect for the divinely given dignity of those to whom we give. This type of charity seeks no recognition, because it is an expression of love which is rooted in our relationship with God.

Our love for God and our love for others are closely interrelated. Genuine love is indivisible. We cannot say that we love God and at the same time neglect those who are known by us to be in need. If our love of God is genuine, the closer we grow to him, the more sensitive we become of the needs of others. The more we sense their pain, the more we want to do for them. The love for God inspires us not simply to be good but to do good for others. If we truly know God to be our Father, then we must also love those other persons who are his sons and daughters.

Saint John Chrysostom speaks boldly about our responsibility to the poor and needy when he says:

> So, give God the honor which he seeks, that is give your money generously to the poor. God has no need of golden vessels but of golden hearts. I am not saying that you should not give golden altar vessels and so on, but I am insisting that nothing can take the place of almsgiving. The Lord will not refuse to accept the first kind of gift but he prefers the second, and quite naturally, because in the first case only the donor benefits, in the second case the poor benefits. The gift of the chalice may be ostentatious; almsgiving is pure benevolence.[4]

While it may seem like a paradox, it is true that the more love which we show for others, the closer we come to God. When we share what we have with the needy and less fortunate especially, we find that we have become the friends of God who seek to emulate his acts of love. Whenever we do something good for the least of the brethren, as the Lord has said, we do it for him (Matthew 25:45).

The Blessing of the Kingdom

Our Lord Jesus Christ declares in the first Beatitude that those who are poor in spirit shall share in the Kingdom of heaven.

The blessing which is promised by the Lord is the experience of God. Those who affirm and who recognize their dependence upon God will be blessed with a share of the Kingdom. For those persons, the reality of the reign of God will not be abstract but rather very immediate. It will not be impersonal. Rather, it will be deeply personal. It will not be only a blessing to be anticipated. On the contrary, it will also be the reality of fellowship with God in the present.

The word "kingdom" as used by Jesus expresses a very important reality. The Greek word, *Basileia*, which is frequently translated as kingdom and the Aramaic word which lies behind it means much more than simply a physical realm or geographical space. The term Kingdom as used by the Lord points to the reign or rule of God. It expressed the immediate, personal, life giving presence of God. When Jesus was speaking of the Kingdom of God or the kingdom of Heaven, therefore, he was not referring primarily to a place but rather to the reality of God's authority and power which is revealed not simply in the age to come but in the present as well.

When we read the New Testament, we see not only that the proclamation of the kingdom is one of the most fundamental characteristics of the teaching of Jesus but also that the Lord spoke of the its rich dimensions.

Jesus began his ministry by declaring that the kingdom was at hand (Mark 1:15) and he went about preaching the "Gospel of the kingdom" (Matthew 4:23). It is given as a gift to those who are willing to change their life receive it (Luke 12:32). So many of the parables express the truth that through Jesus the reign of God has arrived. The stories of the healings and the casting out of demons were signs that the kingdom is being manifested (Matthew 12:28). And, yet there is the sense that the kingdom is not fully revealed in the present (Mark 9:1). The Lord taught his disciples that the kingdom had come upon them and he also directed them to pray for the coming of the kingdom (Matthew 6:10). Jesus taught his followers to seek the kingdom (Matthew 6:33) and assured them that it would grow secretly like a seed (Matthew 13:39). And, Jesus declared that those who are united with him already experience the Kingdom and bear witness to its reality (Luke 12:32).

As we see from only a few references to the Lord's teachings, the reign of God can manifest itself in the lives of faithful believers and in the places where they live. This reign of God is a gift to be received and accepted. God forces himself upon no one. And so, the reign of God – his kingdom – may be experienced by some and not by others. Some may choose to accept and abide by its reality while others may choose to ignore it. The reign may begin like a seed in the life of the believer. And, this seed is already a foretaste of that which is to come when the power of God will be fully revealed and fully perfected. This shall take place both in the life of each of the believers as well as in the entire cosmos. Those who live in accordance with God's reign are blessed and experience the joy of his presence.

Our Lord teaches us in the first Beatitude that the poor in spirit are those who recognize and affirm their ultimate dependence upon God. Those of us who recognize that all our gifts come from our heavenly Father shall know the blessing of the Kingdom of heaven. We shall be happy in the Lord.

From Our Christian Heritage

How are we to come to this humility and leave behind us the deadly swelling of arrogance? By exercising ourselves in it in all things, and by keeping in mind that there is nothing which cannot be a danger to us. For the soul becomes like the things to which it gives itself, and takes the character and appearance of what it does.

Let your demeanor, your dress, your walking, your sitting down, the nature of your food, the quality of your being, your house and what it contains, aim at simplicity. And let your speech, your singing, your manner with your neighbor, let these things also be in accord with humility rather than with vanity. In your words let there be no empty pretense, in your singing no excess sweetness, in conversation be not ponderous or over-bearing. In everything refrain from seeking to appear important. Be a help to your friends, kind to the ones with whom you live, gentle to your servant, patient with those who are troublesome, loving towards the lowly, comforting those in trouble, visiting those in affliction, never despising anyone, gracious in friendship, cheerful in answering others, courteous, approachable to everyone, never speaking your own praises, nor getting others to speak of them, never taking part in unbecoming conversations, and concealing where you may whatever gifts you possess.

Saint Basil the Great[5]

Prayer

We bow our heads to you, O saving Lord, entreating you to accept the offering of our lives just as you accepted the hospitality of your disciples at Emmaus. Stay close to us at all times, and open our hearts to your presence, that, guided by you, we may reach the mansions of your eternal Father together.

For you deserve all glory honor and worship, together with your eternal Father and your all-holy, good, and life-giving Spirit: now and forever, and unto ages of ages. Amen.

Chapter Two

Blessed Are Those Who Mourn
For They Shall Be Comforted

Jesus was once invited by a man named Simon to have dinner at his house (Luke 7:36-50). Simon was a Pharisee. He belonged to the association of men who believed that they were the correct interpreters of the Jewish religious law.

The Pharisees had already begun to make accusations against Jesus because they felt that he was not faithful to the religious laws. Jesus knew that they had accused him of being "a glutton and a drunkard, a friend of tax collectors and sinners" (Luke 8:34). These accusations had been made because Jesus did in fact associate with the sinners and outcasts of the society. To these persons, the Lord spoke with love about the compassion of God the Father.

The Pharisees, on the other hand, avoided contact with such people and based their actions upon their interpretations of the Scriptures. Separating themselves from the poor and needy, the Pharisees appeared to be self-righteous and failed to understand the mercy of God for sinners. Because of this, Jesus had already begun to challenge the hypocritical attitude of the Pharisees by the time Simon issued the invitation (Matthew 7:15-20).

Not long after Jesus sat down at the table, a woman appeared out of nowhere. She was neither an invited guest nor a member of Simon's family. The woman carried an alabaster jar of ointment. As she approached the Lord with tears running down her face, the woman fell to the ground and began to wet the feet of the Lord with her tears. She kissed the feet of the Lord and anointed them with the ointment.

This action of the woman was dramatic. Her tears were at once tears of repentance and joy. They were tears of repentance because she was truly sorrowful for her sins. The fact that she fell at the feet of the Lord was a sure sign that she freely acknowledged her sin and sought the forgiveness of the Lord. Perhaps she was one of those in the crowd who had heard Jesus speaking about the mercy of God. The tears were also tears of joy because she worshipped Christ as the Lord of compassion. Offering the ointment to the Lord was an expression of her gratitude and love.

Simon the Pharisee was indignant over the action of the woman and troubled over the fact that Jesus did not turn her away. Simon said to himself: "If this man were a prophet, he would have known who and what sort of woman this is who is touching him, for she is a sinner" (Luke 7:38). Simon apparently knew the woman to be a prostitute. According to the Jewish law of the day, it was inconceivable that a genuine religious teacher would permit such a person to come near him, let alone touch him.

Jesus knew what was in the heart of Simon. The Lord, however, did not agree with the perspective of Simon. On the contrary, Jesus affirmed both the woman and her action. Honoring both the intent and the deed of the woman, Jesus said to Simon: "Do you see this woman? I entered your house, you gave me no water for my feet, but she has wet my feet with her tears and wiped them with her hair. You gave me no kiss, but from the time I came in, she has not ceased to kiss my feet. You did not anoint my head with oil, but she has anointed my feet with ointment. Therefore, I tell you, her sins, which are many, are forgiven, for she loved much; but he who is forgiven little, loves little" (Luke 7:44-47).

The Lord then turned to the woman and solemnly declared: "Your sins are forgiven." Having heard this, the other people at the table began to say to one another "Who is this that even forgives sins?" But, the Lord paid no attention to their remarks. Again, he spoke to the woman saying: "Your faith has saved you; go in peace" (Luke 7:48-50).

Although he was a member of a group who claimed to understand the actions of God, Simon appears to have been unaffected by the actions and teachings of Christ. Simon failed to honor Christ as the Messiah or to show compassion for the woman who was a daughter of God. The pride and self-righteousness of Simon prevented him from experiencing the mercy of God revealed in Christ.

The woman, on the other hand, appears to have truly grasped the teachings of the Lord although she had sinned. She turned to him with tears of repentance and gratitude. Her humility enabled her to open her heart to God. Through her repentance, she came to experience the mercy of God revealed in Christ. The women honored Christ as the Messiah and gave thanks to him through her actions.

Blessed Mourning

Our Lord Jesus Christ says to us in the second Beatitude: "Blessed are those who mourn for they shall be comforted" (Matthew 5:4).

We can read this Beatitude in two ways. Many of us today may understand mourning primarily in terms of the grief and sorrow associated with the loss of a loved one or with another form of personal tragedy. The biblical accounts depicting the life of Jesus are filled with examples of his compassion toward those who are bereaved. Through these stories, we see various ways the Lord extended the reconciling love, mercy and healing of God to others experiencing loss, pain, and sorrow. Furthermore, we know that he, too was touched personally and profoundly by human grief. We see this through his response to the news of the death of his close friend, Lazarus. "Groaning in spirit" and deeply "troubled," when the Lord was led to the place where his beloved friend Lazarus was entombed, "Jesus wept" (John 11:33-35). Our Lord knew human sorrow deeply, from the inside out.

Today, we can only imagine the difficulties of life experienced by the people who lived during the time of Jesus. Indeed, life was very hard. Tragedy, the death or maiming of loved ones, calamity, the difficulty of earning a day's wages, the double yoke of Roman occupation and the oppression of a judgmental, religious elite, certainly produced enough pain over which persons could mourn. While each of the four gospels, focus considerable attention upon Jesus' responses to these causes of grief, this Beatitude appears to have another meaning to it, according to the ancient tradition of the Church.

When stating "blessed are those who mourn, for they shall be comforted," the Lord teaches that his disciples are persons who mourn over their sins and the sins of others. Sin is not to be celebrated. It is to be mourned. The disciples of the Lord who recognize that we are "poor in spirit" know the tragic consequences of sin. As persons who are created by God to share in his love, we mourn over the fact that sin hardens our hearts. Sin impedes our relationship with God and with others. Sin distorts our identity as daughters and sons of God.

"Blessed mourning" is a healthy attitude of the heart. It exists when we realize at the depths of our being that the dynamics of sin in this world are ultimately more powerful than we are.

We cannot master any sin by our own accord and by personal will power alone. It is only God who can forgive and heal us from sin. God is the one who is more powerful than sin. Genuine regret, or more appropriately, blessed mourning, is the foundation which enables us to leave the sin and cleave to God.

We can describe sin in the following way. It is the free and intentional turning away from God, from his word, and from his service at a particular moment or circumstance. This turning away may take the form of an evil action. It may take the form of an evil word. Indeed, it may even be expressed in the unwillingness to see the truth, to speak the truth or to do what is right and proper. Sin is not only something which we do that is contrary to God. It can also be something which we intentionally do not do. It can be very subtle. Sin can be an intentional act or a lack of action. It can be an intentional evil word or the lack of a good word.

Beneath every sin is a heart which turns away from God. The "heart" in this case does not merely refer to the sentimental seat of the emotions. Rather, Christian spirituality usually identifies the "heart" as the core of the human person. The seat, so to speak, where our deepest intentions, values and priorities abide. Our "heart" is at the core of who we are.

We are created to live in harmony with God and with others. Every form of sin is a distortion of this harmonious way of life. Every sin represents a turning of our heart away from God and toward that which is contrary to him. When we look upon sin in this manner, we see it as something which is not normal to our identity as the sons and daughters of God.

We were not created by our heavenly Father to sin but to share in his goodness and holiness. Therefore, sin is profoundly unnatural. It is contrary to our true self. While we agree with Saint Paul that we all have sinned and fallen short of the glory of God (Romans 3:23), the biblical understanding indicates that sin is a distortion of living. It is a distortion of living which is beneath the dignity of those who are called to follow Christ.

The Path of Repentance

Being faithful to Christ our Lord requires that we recognize those times when we have sinned. Growth in our relationship with the Lord requires that we be honest with ourselves about the manner in which we live our life. While we are called to live our life in fellowship with God, we must recognize that there are times when we have yielded to temptation and have sinned. In so doing, we have fallen short of our vocation to live as sons and daughters of God following the guidance of Christ.

Genuine growth in our Christian life does not result from pretending that we have not sinned. Such a course of action generally leads us to repeat the same sin. Rather, true growth in our relationship with the Lord must take place with the spirit of honest and sincere repentance.

True repentance is a positive process of turning away from sin and back to God. This process is characterized by a clear recognition of our sin, a serious confession of the sin, and a firm resolution to avoid the sin in the future. It involves turning our back upon evil while continuing on with a new discipline of action which helps us overcome our sin through God's mercy. This is essentially the orientation of our heart, that is of our entire life toward God.

The first stage in the process of repentance is our humble and complete recognition of sin. Whether our sin is great or small, the fact remains that every sin does damage to our relationship with God and with others. *Damage occurs even if a sin remains hidden from others and we live otherwise, seemingly "virtu-*

ous" lives. No sin can be viewed as a victory for the work of God. On the contrary, the followers of the Lord who honestly recognize personal sin, ultimately can only mourn over the fact that it has hindered our growth toward God. Every sin tends to weaken our identity as a son or daughter of God.

The second stage of repentance is confession. This means that we must be willing to confess our sin once we have recognized it. Confession means that we honestly acknowledge the sin itself. In other words, we go beyond simply recognizing the error of our ways. We acknowledge the fact that we are accountable for our sin. While the dynamics of sin are greater than we are, our participation in it was also a free act through which we turned away from God, his word, and his service.

The confession of sin may take place in three specific ways. Each way, however, is not distinct from the others but is closely interrelated with the others.

The most fundamental way in which confession of sin may take place is through prayer. So important is this for our growth in Christian life that one of the major expressions of prayer is considered to be a "confession." In our prayer of confession, we have the opportunity to acknowledge before God that we have sinned. Our prayer becomes the means through which we express the concern within us for our sin. As with all types of concerns which are expressed in prayer, our concern over our sin is expressed in a specific manner to God. The prayer of confession is a means of identifying our concern. So, our words of confession before God should always identify the sin, express remorse over it, mourn appropriately for it, and seek the forgiveness of the Father.

Second, many Christians, especially Orthodox and Roman Catholics, also have the opportunity to participate in the special prayer service of confession. This is usually referred to as

"The Sacrament of Confession" or the "Sacrament of Reconciliation." This service is one which is composed primarily of special prayers for the penitent. It is also a prayer service in which the penitent has the opportunity to acknowledge specific sins, especially serious sins which have been very troublesome. The priest, who offers the prayers with the penitent, is present as a witness to the confession. He is also available to offer specific guidance and direction. All of this, of course, is held in the strictest confidence. As the service concludes, the priest, acting in the name of the Lord, pronounces the prayer of absolution. This is a declaration that God is merciful toward the penitent. It is a solemn affirmation that God is the source of recovery and healing.

Third, there may be times when it is appropriate to confess our sin to other trusted believers, especially those who we may have hurt. All sins have a social consequence. In some cases, our sin may do direct harm to another person. In other cases, the harm may be less direct. Yet, regardless of the degree of the sin, every sin, even those which appear to be "private," have an effect upon others.

We are united to others because we all have the same Father. When we do good, others are benefited by our goodness. When we sin, others are harmed. This is the reason why the Apostle James urges us to "confess your sins to one another and to pray for one another" (James 5:16).

If we recognize that our sin has directly harmed a particular person, we can seek an opportunity to go to that person, and to ask for his or her forgiveness. While this may not be easy to do, it is an act of confession which can have a powerful impact upon our relationship with that person. Just as a sin can weaken the relationship between two persons, so also this act of confession can do much to strengthen the bond of love. Seeking the forgiveness of one whom we have hurt can often heal a broken relationship.

Caution is necessary, however. There may be occasions when extending ourselves in this way could expose us or another person to danger or to harm. Not everyone is spiritually or emotionally prepared to receive our honest confession. In these circumstances, it is especially important first to discuss this matter in confidence with another trusted person whom we highly value as being more spiritually mature and healthy than we are. An honest examination of all the circumstances may indicate that it is not appropriate to try directly to seek forgiveness from the one we have sinned against.

We can discern much about the meaning of confession and repentance from the Gospel story of the tax collector named Zacchaeus (Luke 19:1-10). Zacchaeus was a Jew who was appointed to collect the taxes from his own people on behalf of the Romans. He was quite wealthy and had become chief tax collector by the time the event takes place. In order to demonstrate to Jesus his repentance and desire to be forgiven and healed by God, he performs two astounding actions. First of all, he confesses to Christ: "Behold Lord, half of my goods I give to the poor." This bold statement indicates to us how extensive his repentance was. This change effected his very station in society, as well as his relationship with many others whom he did not know.

Second, and perhaps even more astoundingly, he exclaims: "and if I have defrauded any one of anything, I restore it fourfold." The amends made here clearly surpasses the "eye for an eye" expectation typically held in ancient Israel. The restitution paid by Zacchaeus reminds us of the fact that genuine repentance requires, first of all, an unconditional acknowledgment of the evil action which we have done. This is accompanied by a profound, perhaps bordering on lavish, gesture which facilitates healing. Zacchaeus strives aggressively to surpass in goodness the evil which occurred through the injustices against others, as he waited for the mercy of God. And later, the Lord declares this mercy when he proclaims, "Today, salvation has come to this house..." (Luke 19:9).

Regardless of the particular form that it may take, the act of confession is a powerful acknowledgment of the mercy of God. The act of sincere confession is always a prayer spoken with the knowledge that God loves us and cares for each of us. It is not a prayer seeking to avert the anger of God because God is never angry with his beloved sons and daughters. Rather, it is a prayer which affirms a genuine sorrow for sin through which we become distant from our heavenly Father. It is a prayer through which we seek the forgiveness of God for failing to live as his son or daughter. It is also a prayer which affirms that he is the source of healing and recovery.

The final stage of repentance is our resolution not to repeat the sin. If we recognize and confess our sin, we must also be willing to resolve before God that we will do our best with his assistance not to fall into the same sin again.

Our resolution may require that we change certain behaviors or a certain patterns of our life which may have provided the basis for our sin. Often, the circumstances in which we find ourselves create temptations which can lead us into sin. While the temptations themselves are not our sin, we can frequently yield to the temptation. So, in our resolution not to repeat the sin, we must seriously examine the factors which may have contributed to our sin. We must be willing to examine the circumstances, places, and people which may have provided the encouragement for our sin.

This examination may mean that a change in certain routines of our life may be in order if we wish to avoid repeating the same sin. We cannot confess our sin and not be willing to change that which must be altered in our life. In order for us to avoid the occasion for sin, it may be absolutely necessary that we work to alter particular circumstances and responsibilities. It may even be necessary that we alter the relationships which we have with those who may have been associated with our sin.

Our resolution not to repeat the sin can also express itself in some special act of love or generosity. We cannot change the past. But, we can always positively affect the future. The resolution not to fall into sin is also a resolution to live a life which better reflects the teachings of Christ. This means that we may wish to be more deeply conscious of those occasions when we can forgive others, pray for others, speak well of others, and assist those in need.

The process of repentance is one which enables us to experience and to appreciate the mercy of God. Each stage of the process of repentance marks the turning away from sin and a re-orientation of our life toward God. It is a process in which our heart becomes re-centered upon him. It is also a process which more deeply reveals our true identity as a son or daughter of God.

We need to remember that God the Father always keeps the door of repentance open to us. Regardless of the gravity of our sin or the degree of our alienation, we always have the opportunity to turn toward God and seek his forgiveness. There is no sin which cannot be forgiven. Our heavenly Father never abandons us. He waits patiently for our return.

God loves us with a love which has no conditions. He is always ready and willing to receive us even after we have fallen. *His mercy is not contingent upon our repentance. Our repentance, however, enables us to experience his mercy.* Genuine repentance enables us to know God as our loving Father and to draw closer to him.

With this important spiritual truth in mind, Saint John Climacus provides us with a valuable description of the process of repentance when he says:

> Repentance is the renewal of baptism and is contact with God for a fresh start in life. Repentance goes shopping for humility and is ever distrustful of bodily comfort. Repentance is critical awareness and a sure watch over oneself. Repentance is the daughter of hope and the refusal of despair. Repentance is reconciliation with the Lord for the performance of good deeds which are the opposite of sin.[1]

There are two dangers to be avoided when we deal with the past. The first danger is to dwell upon those sins which we have sincerely confessed in the spirit of repentance. Once we acknowledge our past sin before God, we place our trust in his mercy. Because we believe in his forgiveness, we are obliged to put our past sins behind us. If they are truly of the past, then we need not dwell upon them, we need not remember them in an obsessive manner. We need not to be troubled by them. We have acknowledged them once and for all. God has forgiven them and has wiped them away once and for all.

Sometimes, however, many of us will confess something which still haunts us long after the initial confession has been made. We, of course, do not desire this. Perhaps for some of us, it is a compulsive behavior. Perhaps at other times, we may be haunted by the memories of our having been involved in an abusive relationship or situation.

If this is the case, it is necessary to seek the guidance of a spiritual director. The advice of an appropriately skilled spiritual guide is normally essential when we are serious about the process of repentance. This guide can assist us in remembering that God loves us and has forgiven us even though we are still in the process of healing from these traumatic, confusing and, many times guilt ridden memories. In addition to this, a discerning spiritual director would also know how to utilize the varied resources presented by contemporary psychology for the healing of these concerns. A wise spiritual guide may also sometimes encourage us to invite the support of other caring persons who have the experience and professional expertise in helping persons through troubling and traumatic memories.

The second danger is to neglect the serious consequences of sin. As we have said, the sins of the past which we have acknowledged before God need to be firmly placed behind us. We must place our trust in the mercy of God. Yet, at the same time, our recognition of the mercy of God should remind us of the harm which sin can do. There is a lesson to be learned from our past sins. This lesson is the sad reminder that every sin can damage our relationship with God and with others. While we must not obsessively remember the particular sins of the past which we have confessed, we do need to be always mindful of the danger of sin. We must recognize that sin in every form can hurt us and hinder our relationship with God and others.

Saint John of Kronstadt speaks of the importance of centering our lives upon God and of avoiding sin when he says: "The challenge of our life is to be united with God, and sin completely prevents this. Therefore, flee from sin as from the destroyer of the soul. Because to be without God, is death and not life. So, let us understand our goal. Let us always remember that our common master calls us to union with himself."[2]

The Sins of Others

The disciple of the Lord is also called to mourn over the sin of others. To be truly sorrowful over the sin of another person is a profound expression of love. It is for this reason that Saint John Chrysostom says: "They who mourn over their own sins are blessed, but in a less manner. More blessed are they who mourn over the sins of others."[3]

This saying does not diminish the importance of our own need to be sorrowful for our sins. It does remind us, however, that we need to be spiritually attentive to the needs and circumstances of others. If we truly recognize the danger of sin, we can never be happy about its presence either in our own lives or in the lives of other persons.

When Jesus approached the city of Jerusalem for the final time, tears came to his eyes. Although there was great tribulation and pain ahead, the Lord was not weeping for himself. Rather, he was weeping for the people of the city. The word "Jerusalem" means "city of peace." Yet, at that very moment, Jesus sensed the profound lack of peace in the city. He said: "would that even today you knew the things that make for peace. But now they are hidden from your eyes" (Luke 19:41).

Jesus wept for the sins of the people. He wept because he knew that Jerusalem was in fact not a city of peace. He knew all too well the evil, the pride, the arrogance, the hate, and the envy which filled the lives of so many of the citizens. While Jesus certainly did not condone their evil, the Lord wept for the sins of the people. He felt sorrow for the tragic consequences of their sin. He was compassionate for the sinners. As the Son of God who had become fully human, Jesus was without personal sin. Yet, the Lord freely shared in the pain of those who had sinned. He felt the tragedy of those who had become captives of the power of Satan. The Lord felt sorrow for the people whom he had come to save.

Jesus consistently made an important distinction between the sin and the person who sinned. Jesus never condoned sin. He recognized that it was an evil which alienated us from God and from one another. Jesus consistently identified the evil of sin, especially the sins of false pride and hypocrisy. He recognized the tragic consequences of sin in the lives of men and women.

Yet, at the same time, Jesus was able to love the sinner. He refused to condemn the sinner because of the sin. He was able to affirm that the sinner was a person created in the "image and likeness" of God (Genesis 1:26). Despite the gravity of the sin, Jesus treated the sinner as a son or daughter of God. He came into our midst not to condemn the sinners. Rather, as the Lord said, he came as a "physician of the soul" to heal us and to restore us to the love of the Father (Matthew 9:12).

We must learn from the Lord to make the distinction between the sin and the person who sins. Following his example, we must come to condemn sin as an evil. Sin has the power of alienating the sinner from God and from others. It is a tragedy which can truly alter the person's sense of self. But, at the same time, we must also have compassion for the sinner. Regardless of the degree of the sin, the sinner is still a person who is uniquely created by God and loved by him.

Even when we refer to ourselves or to others as "sinners," we do so with the conviction that this is an unnatural state of existence. We are "sinners" because we have freely chosen to behave in a sinful manner. Yet, even when we describe ourselves as "sinners," we are not denying the more fundamental reality that we are unique sons and daughters of God. To designate ourselves or others as being a "sinner," is to describe the state of our existence. It is not a description of our deepest reality. Despite our sins, we never cease to be the sons and daughters of God who are called to live our lives in accordance with his direction and to the glory of his name.

We need to be especially mindful of a very important admonition which the Lord addresses to each of us as we deal with those who have sinned. Jesus says to us: "Judge not lest you be judged, condemn not lest you be condemned, forgive and you will be forgiven." (Luke 6:37). In directing us not to judge or to condemn another person, our Lord is teaching us that we have no right to act as God. We have no right to assume that we can determine the inner character or condition of another person. As we have already said, the Lord God alone is the judge of the human heart. He alone knows the circumstances of each person's life and the motivation behind every person's decisions. The Lord God is the judge.

While we have no right to judge another person, we do, however, have the responsibility to make prudent decisions with regard to the manner in which we shall relate to another person whose behavior is not compatible with the ethics of the Gospel.

Sometimes we may be in a position where we can speak in the spirit of love with a person with regard to his or her sinful behavior. If it is possible and if we are not exposing ourselves or others to danger, we have an obligation to admonish the sinner and to council those who are misled. This is to be done, however, not with a spirit of arrogance or revenge but with a spirit of genuine compassion.

Referring to our responsibility to admonish the sinner in a loving manner, Saint John Chrysostom says:

> Correct him, yes; but not like a foe, an enemy, one out for vengeance, but like a physician administering healing remedies. For the Lord did

not say 'do not restrain the sinner from his sin,'
but, 'do not judge,' – that is, do not be a harsh
judge. For we ought not to condemn or insult
but to admonish; we ought not to slander, but
to council, not to attack in arrogance, but to correct with gentleness and affection. [4]

Let us not forget the difficult fact of human relationships.
Despite our best intentions, we cannot force another person to
change his or her ways. Each of us can only change ourselves.
There are going to be occasions when our loving concern and
caring words can have a powerful impact upon a person who
has been engaged in sinful behavior. There will be other times,
however, when our genuine concern is rejected. Moreover, there
may be occasions when we are simply not in a position to communicate with another person despite our best intentions.

We must remember that we have a responsibility not to condone inappropriate behavior or to expose ourselves or those
we love to the temptation of becoming associated with such
behavior. As Saint Paul reminds us, we are meant to abhor that
which is evil and to cling to that which is good (Romans 12:9).
While not judging the inner character of another person, we
have an obligation to discern the behavior of that person. If we
find that another person's behavior is unacceptable and attempts
at admonition would be dangerous, inappropriate or to no avail,
we have an obligation to separate ourselves from that person
completely, or at least while they are actively engaged in this
behavior, until such time as the behavior ceases. This act of separation must be done in a manner which strives to express a spirit
of genuine love.

There may be some situations where there will be a genuine threat of physical harm, even life-threatening danger if one
person were to approach a more "powerful" person regarding

his or her sinful behavior. This behavior may include domestic violence, spiritual or psychological abuse or financial intimidation.

We must strive to be particularly wise here by refraining from immediately passing judgment upon the "weaker" parties involved. While they too, are fully accountable to God for their inner disposition and behaviors, there are many layers of concern active here. The first is the fact the Church teaches that freedom of will is progressively undermined, proportionately with the rise of intimidation and abuse within these oppressive human relationships and contexts. While nothing and no one can ever completely take away free will, we must deeply appreciate how much more difficult the situations are for the "weaker" parties being abused in these situations. The strength required to seek help on the part of the less powerful must all the more be appreciated and deserves to be recognized and courageously supported by the Church.

An act of separation from a person who is behaving in an inappropriate manner is not an act of rejection or abandonment. We have not ceased to love the other person although we may certainly disapprove of particular behavior. If it can be done in a safe way, we need to communicate clearly that we are ready to reestablish our relationship with the other person when he or she decides to turn away from the sinful activity. This is always our prayer.

Finally, in our dealings with those who have sinned, especially those who have harmed us, we must be cautious that we do not seek to respond in a like manner. Recognizing the sin of another does not give us any right to treat the other person in a sinful manner. It is simply not part of the Christian way of life to return evil for evil. The spirit of vengeance and retribution, while sometimes an understandable human temptation, is still not compatible with the Christian obligation to be compassionate and merciful even to those who wish to harm us. Seeking the assistance of the Lord, the follower of Christ is called to not be overcome by evil but to overcome evil with good (Romans 12:21). In all things, we are called to love the other person. Saint John Chrysostom reminds us that: "Nothing is colder than a Christian who does not care for the salvation of others…. Everyone can be of assistance to his neighbor, if he is willing to fulfill his calling."[5]

The Blessing of Comfort

Our Lord Jesus Christ declares in the second Beatitude that those who mourn shall be comforted.

The experience of the mercy of God is the comfort about which the Lord is speaking. Throughout the teachings of Jesus, he reveals to us that God the Father is merciful. Since God is our loving Father, he does not condemn us when we sin. Rather, he is always ready to receive us back into his fellowship. This does not mean, of course, that God sanctions our sins. He certainly does not. God knows full well that sin is a spiritual disease which harms our relationship with him and others. And, certainly he knows that sin hurts each of us as well.

Yet, while not approving of the sin, God is faithful. He loves the sinner in spite of the sin. Indeed, his mercy is an expression of the fact that each of us belongs to him. When we turn to him with a genuine spirit of repentance, we are able to experience the comfort of his mercy.

In the prayer of the Church, the Holy Spirit is frequently referred to as the "Comforter" (Acts 9:31) This is an important insight because it is the Holy Spirit who enables us to know Christ and to experience the divine mercy and forgiveness which the Lord proclaims in the name of the Father. It is the Holy Spirit who enables us to truly repent and turn our lives toward God and his service.

Regretfully, there is no comfort for those who are unrepentant. When we continue to live in a state of serious sin, our alienation from God and from others produces feelings of guilt. In order to alleviate the discomfort which results from the lack of repentance, we often fall into more serious sins. Indeed, we may try to overcome the discomfort through the abuse of alcohol, drugs, relationships, and sexuality. Such vehicles of escape, however, do not succeed in relieving the discomfort. The fact of the matter is that the abuse of these only compounds our pain.

The sense of brokenness and estrangement which is the product of sin which has not been properly dealt with affects our relationships and responsibilities. Our heart becomes increasingly hardened. We can easily experience a sense of unworthiness. We begin to question our own inherent value and the inherent value of others. We easily begin to feel unloved by God or by others. Finally, we come to despair because we begin to think that even God despises us. Such is the tragic and profound discomfort which can result from sin which is not properly attended to.

God does not force himself or his mercy upon us. We must have the desire to receive his mercy and his healing. The love of God is unconditional. But, we must act in such a way that we can receive his love. For those who mourn over their sin and the sin of others, there is great comfort in the mercy of God. It is a comfort which truly allows us to place our sins behind us and begin anew because of God's love and mercy.

Our Lord teaches us in the second Beatitude that those who mourn over their sins and the sins of others will be comforted. This comfort is the mercy of the Father which comes to us through the presence of the Holy Spirit. It is the experience of God as the source of healing and recovery. We shall be happy in the Lord.

From Our Christian Heritage

Just as the body is clothed in its garments, and the flesh in its skin, and the bones in their flesh, and the heart in its body; so too are we, body and soul, clothed from head to foot in the goodness of God. Yes, and even more closely than that, for all these things will decay and wear out, whereas the goodness of God is unchanging, and incomparably more suited to us. Our Lover desires indeed that our soul should cleave to him with all its might, and ever hold on to his goodness. Beyond our power to imagine does this most please God, and speed the soul on its course.

The love of God most high for our soul is so wonderful that it surpasses all knowledge. No created being can know the greatness, the sweetness, the tenderness of the love that our Maker has for us. By his grace and help, therefore, let us in spirit stand and gaze eternally marveling at the supreme, surpassing, single-minded, incalculable love that God, who is goodness, has for us.

Saint Julian of Norwich[6]

Prayer

O compassionate and merciful Lord, abounding in patience and clemency: Attend to our entreaty and hear the sound of our prayer! Show us some sign of your favor; teach us your ways that we may walk the path of your truth. Give joy to our hearts that we may always revere your holy name, for you are great and you work wonders; you alone are God and there is no other to compare to you, O Lord. You are powerful in mercy and gracious in strength, able and ready to help and comfort and save all those place who their trust in you.

For you deserve all glory, honor, and worship, Father, Son, and Holy Spirit, now and forever and unto ages of ages. Amen.

Chapter Three

Blessed Are the Meek
For They Shall Inherit the Earth

Our Lord taught not simply with the words which he spoke. He also taught through his actions. One of the most dramatic actions of the Lord took place on the night when he met with the disciples for the Last Supper. As they were gathered about the table, Jesus rose and removed his outer garment. He wrapped a towel about his waist. The Lord then poured water into a basin. As the astonished disciples looked on, Christ began to wash their feet.

For the disciples, who knew very well the customs of the ancient Israelites, this action had no precedent. Jesus was by no means their "servant"! He was their Lord and Teacher! So, when Jesus came to Simon Peter, the apostle objected vigorously. "Lord, do you wash my feet?" Peter boldly asked. The Lord patiently responded: "What I am doing you do not know now but afterwards you will understand." But, once again Peter boldly spoke out saying: "You shall never wash my feet." To this, Christ said: "If I do not wash you, you have no part of me." Then, hearing the words of the Lord, Peter apparently recognized the profound significance of the action of the Lord. The apostle then declared: "Lord, not my feet only but also my hands and my head" (John 13:1-9).

After the Lord washed the feet of the Apostles, he reflected upon this action and said: "Do you know what I have done to you? You call me teacher and Lord; and you are right for so I am. If then, your Lord and Teacher has washed your feet, you also ought to wash one another's feet. For I have given you an example, that you also should do as I have done to you" (John 13:12-15).

Christ has truly come as our Lord and our Teacher. In obedience to the will of the Father, the Son of God became incarnate and entered into the very midst of this life. For us and for our salvation, the Word of God "became flesh and dwelt among us" (John 1:14). Because of his love for us, God in the person of Jesus Christ has entered into the very midst of human existence in order to restore us to communion with God our Father.

The coming of the Lord into this world nearly two thousand years ago, however, was not characterized by a great show of prestige and pomp. Christ forced no one to follow him or to abide by his teachings. He compelled no one to follow his example with force or threat. He expressed his teachings not in violence, arrogance or contempt.

On the contrary, the coming of the Lord was characterized by his humble and loving service to others. Although he was, in fact, the promised Messiah who had come to be the light of the world (John 8:12), our Lord came as a humble servant (Luke 22:27). There was no arrogance or haughtiness or contempt in him. He was free from all selfishness and violence. He was gentle and compassionate with others, even with those who sought to persecute him. As the Good Shepherd, he had come to seek and to find the lost sheep. He came willing to lay down his life for those whom he loved (John 10:11).

When we look at the entire story of our Lord's life on earth, his action of washing the feet of the disciples at the Last Supper was not unusual. While it was a dramatic action, it was an action which reflected the very nature of his ministry. The Lord of

Glory entered into this world as one who was "meek and lowly in heart" (Matthew 11:30). By washing the feet of the disciples, Jesus demonstrated that authentic love is always expressed in humble service to others. This is the lesson which he sought to teach his disciples.

A Humble and Contrite Heart

Our Lord Jesus Christ says to us in the third Beatitude: "Blessed are the meek for they shall inherit the earth" (Matthew 5:5).

With these words, the Lord teaches that his disciples are persons who live not only with a sense of dependence upon God but also with a fundamental respect for other persons. We cannot relate with God in isolation from the manner in which we relate with other persons. Such a person abides by the words of the psalm which says: "Trust in the Lord and do what is right; live in the land and enjoy its riches. Find your pleasure in the Lord; he will give you your heart's desire" (Psalm 37 (38) 3-4).

The third beatitude presents us immediately with a special challenge of interpretation. The word "meek" is now generally understood in a manner which is not the one intended by the Lord. Some dictionaries, for example, describe meek as being synonymous with "weak," "submissive," or "frail." As many people use the word today, "meek" has a pejorative meaning. The word is often used in contemporary American English to describe a person who is not courageous or who lacks personal convictions.

Because of this, a number of more recent translations of the New Testament have preferred to use the word "gentle" in place of the word "meek." While this word also may require some measure of interpretation, it does provide us with a further insight into the meaning of the word "meek" as it is used in this

Beatitude as a translation of the Greek word *"pareis."*

When we were children, most of us were taught by our parents to play our games according to the rules. We were taught to respect others. We were also taught that the rules of our games were designed to help us to respect the other players. The rules kept us and others from gaining unfair advantage.

In the course of our childhood games, however, we learned a difficult lesson. This lesson was that not everyone was willing to play in accordance with the rules. There were those who cheated, who bullied, or who lied in order to gain an advantage. Sometimes this unfair advantage not only disrupted the enjoyment of the game but also enabled them to win the game unfairly. This often took place despite the good intentions of the other players.

This difficult lesson of childhood is not forgotten as we grow older. Indeed, the story often repeats itself with only minor variations. This is so because we see that some persons appear to "get ahead" because of their lies, their indiscretions and their threats. So, it is not uncommon for us to see other persons appear to "succeed" in things of this life not because of their goodness, competency, and goodwill toward others. But rather, they appear to "succeed" because they are brash, ruthless, and arrogant.

We also know that some well-intentioned persons are often "stepped upon" by those whose primary concern is their own advancement. Unlike our childhood situations, life is not a game. And, the activities of these self-centered persons can often do damage to others. These self-absorbed persons, unfortunately, have little concern for others.

In the society in which we live, it appears often as though this self-indulgent way of life is the one which is expected of all of us. More often than not, we are advised to be concerned only with our ourselves. Advertisements often give the impression that we are living in a society where selfishness and self-centeredness have become the chief motivation of behavior. Success is frequently defined in terms of power, material acquisitions and social status. Personal rights are frequently affirmed with little regard for personal responsibility or for the legitimate rights of others.

There are some of us who have acquired influence, wealth, prestige, and position not primarily because of our goodness and the proper use of our God-given gifts. Rather, some of us have taken advantage of others. Often we have forgotten God and we have failed to respect the inherent dignity of others. We have neglected our responsibility to be honest and just. Some of us have lived our lives neither to honor God nor to serve others. Some of us have lived only for ourselves and our acquisitions. We have sought some type of self-defined "success" at any cost.

This is not the way of life which the Lord expects us to live. He wants his followers to live a life which is fully and authentically human. This means that the disciples of the Lord are called to affirm honestly that we are dependent upon God for all that we are and for all that we have. The disciples of the Lord are also called to be tolerant and gentle in our dealings with others. In both our relationship with God the Father and in our dealings with others, we are called to imitate the example of Christ.

Saint Basil the Great reminds us that our Lord presents us with an example to be followed when he says:

> Every act and every word of our Savior Jesus Christ is a guide for piety and virtue. For this reason, he became human so that in images he might depict both piety and virtue for us, and so that every man and woman might look upon

and strive after the prototype. For this reason, he bears our body so that we may imitate his life.[1]

The Good Samaritan

Perhaps one of the most important stories which the Lord taught us is the parable of the Good Samaritan (Luke 10: 25-37). It is a powerful story which expresses the fundamental character of love which is sacrificial and free from all selfishness.

The story was taught by the Lord in response to a question. A young man had come to Jesus and asked the Lord what had to be done in order to inherit eternal life. The man was asking the Lord what was required to live in fellowship with God both now and in the age to come. The man was not concerned with "success" but rather with salvation. Knowing this, Jesus answered the question by asking the young man what was written in the Law of Moses. The man, who was a student of the Scriptures, replied by saying: "You shall love the Lord your God with all your heart, and with all your soul, and with all your strength, and with all your mind; and your neighbor as yourself." The Lord then said to him: "You have answered right; do this and you will live " (Luke 10:26-28).

The young man, however, was apparently not satisfied. He then asked: "And who is my neighbor " (Luke 10:29)? The question may have been a challenge to the teaching authority of Jesus. But, the question may have also reflected a debate among students of the Law of Moses in those days. There were many who had a very narrow understanding of "neighbor." For these persons, the term "neighbor" applied only to someone who was a fellow believer or a fellow countryman. A "stranger" could not be considered as a neighbor. And because of this, a "stranger" did not have to be treated properly. So, Jesus was being asked to indicate how he would interpret the commandment to love one's neighbor.

Responding to the question, Jesus told the story of a man who while traveling from Jerusalem to Jericho. The man was set upon by robbers. After robbing the man, the bandits stripped him, beat him, and left him unconscious on the road.

Two persons passed by the victim of the robbers. The first was a priest from the Temple. Although he was one of the leaders of the worship services in the Temple and certainly knowledgeable of the Law of Moses, the priest passed by the man in need. The second was an administrator in the Temple who was known as a Levite. Like the priest, he knew well the rituals of worship and the Law of Moses. Yet, the Levite also ignored the unconscious man on the road.

The third person to come upon the man in the road was a Samaritan. Living in the region of Samaria, these people were a considered to be heretics and despised as "half-breeds" by many Israelites, especially the Pharisees. Unlike the priest and the Levite, however, the Samaritan did not ignore the wounded man on the road. The traveler bandaged the wounds of the victim and brought him to a nearby inn. There, the Samaritan instructed the innkeeper to take care of the man's needs and promised to pay whatever it would cost.

When Jesus completed the story, he asked the young man: "Which of these three, do you think, proved neighbor to the man who fell among the robbers?" The young man replied: "The one who showed mercy to him." And Jesus said to him, "Go and do likewise" (Luke 10:36-37).

Our Lord taught through this parable an important lesson about love and our responsibility to others. He refused to accept a narrow definition of "neighbor." Christ recognized and affirmed that every human person is worthy of respect and love. Respect and love are not to be offered only to those persons whom we know, or only to those persons who share our convictions, or only to those who are of our racial background, social class, or to those who share our religious beliefs. While the priest and the Levite ignored their responsibilities, the Samaritan responded in love to his neighbor whom he found in need. The Samaritan was truly a person who trusted in God and did what was right (Psalm 37:3).

Jesus did not give to us a detailed guidebook which discusses every possible event which could occur in our lives. This was not his intent. Yet, the Lord did clearly teach us about our obligation to love God and to love our neighbor as ourselves. He provided us with numerous examples of how this love can be expressed. By carefully listening the words of Christ and by carefully observing his actions, we can find much guidance in living our life as his followers. We do this with confidence that he continues to be with us as the Risen Lord who offers us his guidance in the present.

Relationships of Love

Our Lord clearly identified the chief characteristics of the disciple's relationship with him when he said. "You shall love the Lord your God with all your heart, and with all your soul, and with all your mind; this is the first and great commandment. And the second is like it, you shall love your neighbor as yourself" (Matthew 22:37-39). According to these words of the Lord, the follower is one who loves God, and others and self. These three expressions of love are intimately related.

We must look to the love which God shows for us in order to gain insight into the quality of love about which the Lord speaks. Speaking of the character of divine love, Saint Paul tells us: "God shows his love for us in that while we were yet sinners Christ died for us" (Romans 5:8).

With these simple words, we are reminded that the love of

God for us is his desire for our well being and happiness. This love is not dependent either on our worthiness or upon our ability to respond. It is love which is freely given. It is love which is sacrificial. It is love which is unconditional. It is love which seeks no reward for the lover but always seeks the good for the beloved. God's love is freely offered to all. It is a love through which he wholly identifies himself with every person.

Throughout his ministry, Christ reveals in very concrete ways the love of God. Because of his love, Christ identifies himself with us and freely accepts the limitations of human existence. It is because of love that he casts out demons. It is because of love that he heals the sick. It is because of love that he raises the dead. It is because of love that he forgives the sinner. It is because of love that he proclaims the Gospel in both word and deed, and is willing even to give his life for the sake of our salvation. The Lord himself says: "Greater love has no man than this, that a man lay down his life for his friends" (John 15:13).

Saint Nicholas Cabasilas expresses the infinite love of God for us when he says:

> God pours himself out in an ecstasy of love. He does not remain in the Heavens and call to himself the servant he loves. No, he himself descends and searches out for such a servant, and comes near, and lets his love be seen, as he seeks what is like himself. From those who despise him, he does not depart; he shows no anger toward those who defy him, but follows them to their very doors, and endures all things, and even dies, in order to demonstrate his love. All this is true, but we have not yet declared the highest things of all: for not merely does God

enter into close fellowship with his servants and extend to them his hand, but he has given himself wholly to us, so that we are become temples of the living God, and our members are the members of Christ. The head of these members is worshipped by the cherubim, and these hands and feet are joined to that heart.[2]

Love of God

We are called by the Lord to love God with our whole heart, our whole soul, and our whole mind (Matthew 22:37). In using the words "heart, soul, and mind," Jesus is emphasizing that we are meant to love God completely. Our entire self is meant to respond to God in love. All of our actions and our thoughts are meant to be rooted in our love for God. When we love God in this way, we seek to identify our entire self with him. We want his goodness to be our goodness. We want his will to become our will. We want his actions to become our actions.

This means that our love for God necessarily manifests itself in a number of basic and interrelated ways. Our love for God manifests itself in our desire to know him, to love him and to serve him in every aspect of our life. Our love for God manifests itself in our worship of him. It is through worship that we affirm that he is the source of all. Our love for God manifests itself in our prayer to him. It is in prayer that we profess our dependence upon him and open ourselves to his presence. Our love for God manifests itself in our loving concern for others. It is in loving others that we not only follow his commandment but also become the mediators of his love in the world.

We are meant to love God and to share in his life. It is natural for us to be drawn to him because he is our Father and the source of our life. He has given each of us the potential to love.

This is the conviction which Saint Basil expresses when he says:

> The love of God is not something we learn from another. Neither did we learn from another how to love the sunshine or how to defend our life. Nor has anyone taught us how to love our parents, or those who have reared us. And so, indeed much more, learning to love God does not come from outside. But in the very commencement of the life of the person there is placed within us a certain seminal conception which has from itself the beginnings of all a natural propensity towards this love.[3]

These words of Saint Basil are quite significant. He affirms the fact that it is natural for us to love God and to live in communion with him. As human persons, we are "God oriented" from the very moment of our personal creation. We have an innate desire to love God which is essential to our identity as a human person.

Love of Neighbor

We are also called by the Lord to love our neighbor as ourselves. It is important to note how closely the Lord links the love of God with the love of neighbor. Clearly, this means that we cannot claim to love God unless we love our neighbor. In a very real sense, love has an indivisible character about it. The more we truly love God the more we shall love others. And, likewise, the more we love others the greater we shall love God.

There is a relationship between the love which we have for God and the love which we have for others. As we draw closer to God in love, the more closely we are drawn in love to others. The intimate relationship between our love for neighbor and our love for God is emphasized by Saint Dorotheus of Gaza when he says:

Imagine a circle marked on the ground. Suppose that this circle is the world, and that the center of the circle as God. Leading from the edge of the circle to the center are a number of lines, and these represent the paths or ways of life that people can follow. In their desire to come closer to God, the saints move along these lines towards the middle of the circle, so that the further they advance, the nearer they approach both God and to one another. The closer they come to God, the closer they come to one another, and the closer they come to each other, the closer they come to God.[4]

Such is the nature of love. The nearer we draw to God in our love for him, the more we are united together by love for our neighbor. The greater our union with our neighbor, the greater is our union with God.

Throughout his teachings and especially in the parable of the Good Samaritan, Jesus shows us very clearly that our neighbor should not be narrowly defined as the person who lives next to us. Furthermore, our neighbor is not simply the person who shares our faith, or who is of our race, or who speaks our language, or who is of our social class. Jesus refuses to accept a rather narrow definition of neighbor which limits also our responsibility to love. On the contrary, according to the perspective of Jesus, our neighbor is any person – and especially a person who is in need.

We are called to love our neighbor in a manner which reflects the love which God has for us and which is revealed powerfully in the life of Christ. Following the example of the Lord, our love for the other person bears witness to the fact that he or she is a son or daughter of God. Every person belongs to

God and is graced with his "image and likeness" (Genesis 1:26).

Our love for the other, therefore, will always respect this fundamental personal identity and inherent value. Love treats every person as a "person" and not as an inanimate object. Our love for them will be one which expresses a profound concern for their good and well-being. Having this sacrificial character, it will be a love which is freely given without expectation of anything in return.

In his first letter to the Corinthians, Saint Paul provides a classic description of love as it is understood by Christians. He says:

> If I speak in the tongues of men and of angels but have not love, I am a noisy gong or a clanging cymbal. And if I have prophetic powers and understand all mysteries and all knowledge, and if I have faith, so as to remove mountains, but have not love, I am nothing. If I give away all I have and if I deliver my body to be burned but have not love I gain nothing.
>
> Love is patient and kind; love is not jealous or boastful; it is not arrogant or rude. Love does not insist on its own way; it is not irritable or resentful; it does not rejoice at wrong, but rejoices in the right. Love bears all things, believes all things, hopes all things, endures all things. Love never ends (1 Corinthians 13:1-8).

Love for Self

We cannot conclude these reflections on love without discussing one final concern. It is very important for us to recognize that the Lord says that we must love our neighbor "as ourselves." Clearly, Jesus expects here, that we do indeed have love for our own self.

This is not meant to be the self-centered or self-absorbed concern which often passes for "self love." On the contrary, it is a healthy respect for our own self which is reflective of our identity and our relationship to God. It is not love "of self." Rather, it is a genuine love "for self." This authentic love "for self" is one which recognizes the love which God has for each of us, the dignity only he can bestow on us and the gifts which he has given to each of us. It is a love "for self " which affirm that each of us is valuable to him.

We are able to have love "for self" because God loves us as his children. Speaking of the dignity which we enjoy as the sons and daughters of God, Saint Gregory of Nyssa says:

> For this is the safest way to protect the good things you enjoy: Realize how much your Creator has honored you above all other creatures. He did not make the heavens in his image, nor the moon, the sun, the beauty of the stars or anything else which surpasses understanding. You alone are a reflection of eternal beauty, a receptacle of happiness, an image of the true light. And, if you look at him, you will become what he is, imitating him who shines within you, whose glory is reflected in your purity. Nothing in the entire creation can equal your grandeur. All the heavens can fit into the palm of the hand of God... Although he is so great that he can hold all creation in his palm, you can wholly embrace him. He dwells within you.[5]

These remarkable words of Saint Gregory remind us of our dignity and honor which are rooted in God and his love. God has first loved us. God has first honored us. Our challenge is to recognize this truth and to live our lives accordingly.

Many of us may have a difficult time in expressing love "for self." We often perceive ourselves as persons without intrinsic value. At a very deep level of awareness, some of us may even reject our own selves. On a number of occasions, this may be the product of surviving inappropriate adult relationships and expectations while we were growing up. Knowingly or unknowingly, these persons somehow taught us "truths" about ourselves which may or may not have been connected with God's reality. As a result, certain needs related to healthy growth may have been left unattended. It is a sad and painful fact that, in too many of our homes and communities, these unattended needs have hardly been acknowledged. In certain contexts, this may have been a form of "passive" neglect and abuse.

Let us be clear here that, as we briefly consider abuse here, we are not referring to the sometimes "roller coaster," difficult and negative times which beset most healthy families from time to time. One of the beauties and challenges of life, is that it is unpredictable. Furthermore, no one person, family, community or society is "perfect." Only God is perfect. In fact, unpredictable challenges occurring in a fairly healthy family typically become opportunities to work difficult issues through to a deeper level of authentic living, with the help of God. Nevertheless, growing up in a healthy family situation is not supposed to help us escape our coming face to face with our own personal, adult-sized vulnerabilities, limitations and sins. With the help of God, these need to be courageously faced, confessed and healed. In a manner far beyond our human understanding, the Lord desires to assist us with developing a healthy love "for self" as we endeavor to grow closer to him.

Having said this, we must also recognize that there are a number of good people who have also been actively abused as children, adolescents or even adults. This may have taken the form of sexual, physical, financial or emotional abuse, intimidation or neglect. It is not unusual for a combination of these to occur. Abuse manifests itself in many forms and degrees of intensity. While stories vary in every given situation, the consequences of damage related to the psyche of these survivors can be far reaching, even devastating.

Those of us who had no choice but to grow up in these contexts were victimized by the neglect, negativity, destructive behavior or violence of other persons through no fault of our own. Some of us may still feel guilty and even ashamed because we feel that we somehow "attracted" this behavior from the persons who injured us.

As a result of this process, our own sense of self-esteem suffers at least two types of serious damage. First of all, we often experience ourselves to be unacceptable in the eyes of God and others. Some of us feel like a "fake" or "fraud" in the presence of those around us. A sense of on-going shame or humiliation seems to surround our being, and we try to fight this in various ways.

We continually have a difficult time in valuing our own self. While those of us who grew up in fairly happy homes may occasionally feel this way in certain situations, those of us who had to contend with more difficulties may experience these feelings more persistently, more acutely and in more numerous situations. These are spiritually and psychologically debilitating experiences. A smaller number of us may even accept these hopeless, God-effacing, "I am bad" messages *to the core of our being*. Some may sometimes begin to behave in a reciprocally "bad" manner, perhaps as a way to defiantly "fight back."

Second, even if "bad" behaviors do not appear to take root, adequate opportunities to discover, appreciate and develop many of the positive, healthier parts of our unique personhood simply do not always occur. *This may also happen even when the family is healthy.* Sometimes, what every person needs, as this ultimately originates mysteriously with God, cannot be discerned from within the family, as such. Thus, it becomes difficult to express love "for self" as certain positive life experiences are lacking. Instead of knowing that we need to seek God and learn from these life experiences, with the help of God, we wrongly came to see our own self as unworthy of being loved by God and others. We came to believe that we have little to no good to offer.

As we grew older, many of us developed unhealthy coping mechanisms in order to survive these negative beliefs and feelings. We developed harmful and self-defeating relationships with other people, alcohol, drugs, work, money, success, possessions, food or sex. These attempts to gain power over these painful aspects of life easily took on a progressively negative reality of their own. While these mechanisms in the beginning may have helped us in some manner survive less acceptable situations, the more we depended upon these mechanisms, the more inappropriate our relationship with them became. While these mechanisms may have originated with somewhat noble intentions, these too come to betray us. Sadly, these "escape routes" eventually cause only destruction in our lives, compounding the situation in the long run.

So, growing up even in healthy families, usually does not protect us for having to come face to face with our own personal adult vulnerabilities. In every one of these situations, the Lord desires to assist us with developing a healthy love "for self." In order to do so, it is usually necessary for us to seek the guidance of a discerning spiritual director. Sometimes, we may also desire to invite the assistance of a skilled counselor in helping us discern how to take action against these harmful coping mechanisms.

We can benefit from the insights of caring "healthier-than-we-are" friends, and friends who desire healthy relationships. These persons could be more available to us in the frequent common and daily challenges we face. These persons can assist us in gaining a better perspective on our past, in affirming our value and fundamental goodness as unique human persons created in the "image and likeness" of God, and in discerning more appropriate responses to the present day challenges we face.

A healthy and legitimate love "for self" is essential for our development. Because God has created us, each of us is of ultimate value. Unless we have the proper regard for our self, it becomes very difficult to experience fully the love of God or to share fully that love with others. Our love "for self" is realized, however, not in isolation from God but in communion with him. It is a love which is sustained not in opposition to other persons but in harmony with them.

Saint Macarius of Egypt reminds us of our dignity through our intimate relationship with God when he says:

> Look how mighty are the heavens and the earth, the sun and the moon. But it was not in these that the Lord rested. The human person, therefore, is of more value than all creatures, and I dare say he is more valuable that any creature, visible or invisible, more valuable than the ministering angels. When God said: 'Let us make man in our image and after our likeness,' he was not speaking of the Archangels Michael and

Gabriel. He was speaking about the spiritual substance of the human person, his immortal soul.[6]

The Blessing of Inheriting the Land

Our Lord Jesus Christ declares in the third Beatitude that those who are meek shall inherit the earth.

The blessing about which the Lord speaks is not to be understood primarily as a tangible plot of land. Rather, he is saying that those persons who are meek and gentle and, thereby, live their lives faithfully will be provided with all they need. God does not forget those who depend upon him. He provides them with the blessings which stand the test of time.

With this Beatitude, Jesus is reminding us that the true blessings of life are not gained by those who are ruthless and arrogant. Yes, these people may acquire many things in this life through their disreputable manner of living. But, there acquisitions are transitory and not satisfying because they fail to recognize the God who is the source of all.

God cares for his faithful daughters and sons. He does not abandon us in time of need. He knows us well. As the loving Father, he not only cares about us but also he provides us with what is necessary in our growth in holiness. Thus, it is not the arrogant, who are faithless, who will inherit the earth. Rather, it is the meek and gentle, who are faithful. They shall inherit the earth. They shall rejoice in the blessings of God.

Our Lord teaches us in the third Beatitude that the meek are blessed. Those of us who are gentle in our dealings with others will receive all that we need from God for our growth in holiness. We shall be happy in the Lord.

From Our Christian Heritage

Love is the foremost of all excellent achievements and the first of the commandments of the Law. Love is the life of God, and it cannot be otherwise, since perfect beauty is necessarily lovable to those who recognize it; and out of this recognition comes love. The insolence of abundance cannot touch this perfect beauty, nor can abundance ever put a stop to man's power to love what is entirely beautiful; and so the life of God consists in the eternal practice of love; and this life is wholly beautiful, possessed of a loving disposition toward beauty and never receiving any check in the practice of love. And because beauty is boundless, love shall never cease.

St. Macrina[7]

Prayer

O God, faithful and true, who are merciful thousands upon tens of thousands of times with those who love you, O friend of the lowly and protector of the poor, O you whom all things need because they are all subject to you: Look on your people as they bow their heads to you, and bless them with a spiritual blessing. Guard them as the apple of your eye, preserve them in piety and justice, and make them worthy of eternal life.

For you are one to have mercy on us and to save us, O God, and we give you glory, Father, Son, and Holy Spirit: now and forever, and unto ages of ages. Amen.

Chapter Four

Blessed Are Those Who Hunger and Thirst For Righteousness For They Shall Be Satisfied

One day Jesus was passing through the village of Jericho which is located about ten miles northeast of Jerusalem. Wherever the Lord went, a crowd usually gathered about him. And, the visit of the Lord to this village was no exception. As he walked along the road, people surrounded him. Some people were simply curious. They wanted to get a look at the person whom many claimed was the Messiah. Others in the crowd were more than curious. They were anxious to hear the teachings of Jesus. Perhaps they even wanted to believe that he truly was the Messiah. Perhaps they wanted to become his followers.

One of the citizens of Jericho was Zacchaeus (Luke 19:1-10). He was a wealthy man who earned his living as a tax collector. This meant that he was probably not very well liked by his neighbors. In those days, the tax collectors in Palestine were not held in very high esteem because they were usually Jews who worked for the Roman Government. The tax collectors also had a reputation for being corrupt civil servants. So, many other Jews, especially those who strictly interpreted the Mosaic Law, would have nothing to do with a person such as Zacchaeus. He was viewed as being "impure" because he worked for the Romans.

Zacchaeus wanted to see Jesus during the Lord's journey

through Jericho. Not being very tall, Zacchaeus could not see over the heads of the people who surrounded Jesus as he walked through the village. But, Zacchaeus was undaunted. He ran ahead of the crowd and climbed up a sycamore tree. There, in the branches of the tree, he sat like a little boy as he waited for the Lord to pass by.

As Jesus approached the tree, he saw Zacchaeus. And the Lord said to him: "Zacchaeus, make haste and come down; for I must stay in your house today" (Luke 19:5).

The tax collector's courage and persistence were rewarded. Zacchaeus climbed down from the tree and led Jesus into his house. When some other people saw this, however, they began to gossip. They began to say to each other that Jesus had gone to be a guest in a house of a person whom they called a sinner. With this remark not only were they judging Zacchaeus but also they were criticizing the Lord for spending time with a person who was a tax collector.

Zacchaeus received the Lord into his house with great joy. Perhaps knowing of the false accusations which were made against him, the tax collector declared: "Behold Lord, half of my goods I give to the poor; and if I have defrauded anyone of anything, I restore it fourfold."

Jesus then said to him: "Today, salvation has come to this house, since he is also a son of Abraham. For the son of man came to seek and to save the lost" (Luke 19:8-10).

The longing of Zacchaeus to see Jesus was fulfilled. Indeed, not only did Zacchaeus see the Lord but also he was gifted with a relationship with Christ and with all those who were associated with Christ.

To Hunger and Thirst for God and His Righteousness

Our Lord Jesus Christ says to us in the fourth Beatitude:

"Blessed are those who hunger and thirst for righteousness for they shall be satisfied" (Matthew 5:6).

The word righteousness is not one commonly used today. At first glance, we might be prone to substitute the words virtue, justice, or right living as appropriate synonyms. These words help us to gain a certain insight into one aspect of the meaning of righteousness. At the same time, we also have to recognize that "righteousness" is a scriptural word which has a number of interrelated aspects. Firstly, it points to God who is truly the Righteous One (Psalm 24:8). It then bears witness to the saving relationship which the Living God offers us through Christ. It also reminds us that the followers of Christ are called to live their lives in a manner which bears witness to the Lord and his teachings. Jesus seems to have brought all of these together when he directed his followers to seek first God's Kingdom and his righteousness (Matthew 6:33).

With this Beatitude, the Lord teaches us that his disciples are persons who seek after God, the God who first seeks us. God is the one who is truly righteous. Because the source of our existence is beyond our self, there is in each of us an inclination to transcend the limitations of self. It is the tendency toward perfect union with the One who is the source of our lives. As persons created in the "image and likeness" of God (Genesis 1:26), we have an innate orientation towards the One who created us. We have a inner longing to know, to love, and to serve God, and an inner desire to live in fellowship with him. We must follow our inner longing for God and do what we must in order to grow closer to him. Our life is meant to be a total response to his presence and his love.

The Psalmist has captured the spirit of this longing when he says: "As a doe longs for running streams, so does my soul long for you, O my God. My soul thirsts for God, the living

God. When can I begin to enjoy the presence of God" (Psalm 42 [41]: 1-2).

The proper object of this intense longing, however, is not the things which are sought so ardently by some of us. Often, we crave wealth, power, prestige, popularity as well as those tangible effects which symbolize and even embody these objects of intense desire. We are often fooled into believing that these "things" will satisfy our longing and bring a sense of satisfaction to our lives.

In a distorted understanding of our life, the gifts of God can detract us from God. When we fail to recognize the ultimate source of our blessings, his gifts can become our "idols." These "idols" can become for us very imperfect substitutes for God. These become what has been often called in ancient Christian literature, "attachments." And, we often find ourselves craving these attachments rather than longing for the God who is beyond all idolization.

While the longing of the human spirit to transcend itself is real, the transitory objects of our craving do not bring genuine satisfaction. The human inclination to reach beyond the confines of self is not satisfied for very long by our "attachment" to idols. Sadly, substituting our desire for God with a craving for idols can lead to one tragedy after another. These idols are never fully satisfying and so in time they become "gods" of tyrannical proportions. Likewise, addictions to various substances and unhealthy behaviors also become tyrannical idols which do not provide true satisfaction. Yet, these afflict many of us and are real maladies to which attention must be given.

Viewed from a deeper perspective, our inappropriate attachments as well as our addictions are symptoms of a longing for God which has been distorted. This distortion can only lead to greater brokenness because the human spirit which longs for the joy of wholeness in union with God has not found the proper object of its quest.

At the very beginning of his autobiography, Saint Augustine of Hippo in Africa expresses well the fundamental reality of the human condition. He says in his prayer to God: "You have made us for yourself and our heart is restless until it rests in you." [1] The restlessness of the heart about which the saint speaks is the longing to be united with God in a conscious manner. Not only has God created us but also he has created us to live in fellowship with him in this life and in the life to come. It is natural for us to live in fellowship with God. And, it is profoundly unnatural for us to live our lives separated from God. Until we live our life in fellowship with God, we are living with a "restless heart" in a manner which is not complete. We are living a life which is ultimately less than human.

Saint Augustine had come to appreciate this truth after many years of restlessness. A person of great intellectual ability, he lived a life as a young adult which was characterized both by philosophical studies and by hedonism. Yet, as he eventually acknowledged, neither his studies nor his hedonism brought to him genuine satisfaction or a sense of wholeness. In the years prior to his conversion to Christianity, he had abused the gifts which God had given to him. His longing for wholeness was genuine. But, the objects of his longing were false. Saint Augustine was truly a restless young man until he found the genuine object of his longing.

Through the prayers of his devout mother, Saint Monica, and the wisdom of Saint Ambrose, the bishop of Milan, the restless Augustine eventually recognized the folly of his ways. He came to see that God was the true object of his longing and he became a follower of Christ.

The Divine Gift of a Saving Relationship

This Beatitude reminds us that God, the truly Righteous One, offers to us a relationship with him. This relationship is an expression of God's love.

Christians believe that God wills that all be saved and come to a knowledge of his truth (1 Timothy 2:4). God wants each of us to live in his presence as full and authentic human persons. To be saved, therefore, means both to be rescued by God in Christ from the power of sin which dehumanizes us and to be enabled to live in harmony with God the Father by sharing in his fellowship. It is through living in harmony with God that we become most fully human. Salvation, therefore, is not something which we can achieve through our merits alone. Rather, it is first and foremost a gift which the Father freely offers to us in Christ and through the Spirit. Our heavenly Father wills first of all that we come to know him, love him, and serve him. He offers to us a relationship of love.

Christ has come among us as the bearer of salvation. Through his life, death, and resurrection, the Lord has dramatically revealed the depth of the Father's love for us. As Saint John tells us: "For God so loved the world that he gave his only Son, that whoever believes in him should not perish but have eternal life. For God sent the Son into the world, not to condemn the world, but that the world might be saved through him" (John 3:16-17). Christ has come because of the Father's love for us. Through his life, death and resurrection, Jesus reveals to us the reality of God and our own true identity as daughters and sons of God.

Christ has united in his person divinity with our human nature. Through his words, Christ has revealed to us the truth about God and ourselves. And, through his death and resurrection, Christ has conquered the power of evil once and for all.

In every aspect of his life, the Lord has revealed to us the power of God's love. With Saint Paul, we affirm that Christ is "the power of God and the wisdom of God." He has become "our wisdom, our righteousness and sanctification and redemption" (1 Corinthians 1:24, 30)

Although we live nearly twenty centuries after the Lord taught in Galilee, he is not a distant figure of history. The Risen Lord is alive and present in our midst as he promised (Matthew 28:20). Today, he calls us to follow him and make the gift of salvation our own. Fellowship with God our heavenly Father is offered to us through the Risen Lord who continues to act through the Spirit to lead us to the Father.

Salvation is a gift from God. Yet, it is not a gift which is imposed upon us in an arbitrary manner. God does not compel us to accept this gift. He does not force us to love him. He does not oblige us to abide in his truth. While we are intimately related to him through our creation, God never disregards the fact that we are free either to choose him or to reject him. He has not created impersonal robots. On the contrary, he has created men and women who are endowed with the freedom of choice. Each of us has the opportunity either to reject God or to respond to God by accepting the gift of salvation which he offers to us in Christ.

While salvation is a gift, it is also a gift which must be realized in our own life through a personal relationship with God the Father through the Risen Christ and in the Spirit. We must do our part to respond to him. He is always the focal point of salvation. Although the Lord offers to us a relationship of love, we must be willing to accept this relationship and to cultivate it. It is a gift which must be sought after and made our own by living in communion with him. As the Son of God, Christ shares himself with us so that we might share ourselves with him in a loving relationship. By coming to share our life with him, we make the gift of salvation our own.

In his commentary on the Gospel of Saint John, Saint John Chrysostom reminds us that God does not compel anyone to be his servant. He says:

> Since God loves human beings and is benefi-
> cent, he does what he can so that we may radiate
> virtue. God wants us to win glory, and because
> of this he does not draw anyone by force or con-
> straint. Rather, God attracts by persuasion and
> kindness all those who are willing to respond,
> and so wins them over. Some, therefore received
> him when he came, while others did not. God
> wishes to have no servant who is unwilling or
> who is forced into service. God wants all to come
> of their own free will and choice, and with grati-
> tude to him for this grace.[2]

Christ emphasizes our responsibility in making this relationship work when he tells us in the fourth Beatitude that we
must hunger and thirst for righteousness. The Lord is teaching
us here that we have a responsibility for cultivating our relationship with him. We must respond to his presence. We must
seek the righteousness of God which is centered upon the gracious relationship brought about through Jesus Christ. He is
the light. But, we must accept the light (John 8:12). He is the
way, the truth and the life (John 14:6). But we must accept him
as our way, our truth, and our life. We must sincerely "hunger
and thirst" for Christ who is the bread of life and the living
water of salvation (John 6:35, 7:28).

The relationship between each of us and the Lord is a dy-
namic one which has a beginning but which has no ultimate
end. Its genesis is the very moment that we are conceived in

our mother's womb. From the moment that we come into existence, we do so because of God's creative love. We are his and we belong to him from the first moment of our existence. It is with our baptism that this relationship becomes a public one which is centered upon the person of Christ. The bond between ourselves and the Lord which was hidden from the time of our creation becomes manifest by means of our public identification with Christ and with his Church through the sacrament of baptism. As Christ publicly identified himself with us by his baptism in the Jordan River, so also do we publicly identify ourselves with Christ through our baptism.

Each of us must become like Zacchaeus. We must be ready and willing to do our part in responding to the presence of the Lord. From the time of our baptism, the bond of love between the Lord and each of us is nurtured in a special way by the Holy Spirit in so far as we are willing to open our lives to the presence of the Lord.

Each time we pray, this relationship with Christ is given nourishment through the Spirit. Each time we receive Holy Communion, this relationship with Christ is strengthened through the Spirit. Each time we read the Scriptures, this relationship with Christ is given direction through the Spirit. Each time we love another, this relationship with Christ is enriched through the Spirit. In all the responsibilities and relationships of our life, the Spirit is present to aid is in becoming more deeply united with Christ and conformed to his likeness.

Because our relationship with the Lord is one of love, it need never end. It has the potential of always growing deeper and richer provided that we choose not to turn away from the Lord. Even death itself does not destroy this relationship which we have with the Lord but simply alters its context. For those who believe in Christ, death is not the end of existence.

Rather, death is a passage into a new manner of existence in which our distinct identity will be preserved. On the other side of death, we continue to have the opportunity to know, love, and serve God the Father through our relationship with Christ. Both in this life and in the life to come, we have the opportunity to "grow from one degree of glory to another" through our relationship with Christ and those others who are in Christ (2 Corinthians 2:18).

Saint Gregory of Nyssa builds upon the observation of the Apostle Paul when he says:

> So he teaches us, I think, that in our constant participation in the good, the graces which we receive at every point are indeed great. But, the path which lies beyond our immediate grasp is infinite. This will constantly happen to those who truly share in the divine goodness: They will always enjoy a greater and greater participation in grace throughout all eternity. [3]

The saving relationship which God offers to us through Christ has often been described as a process of "theosis," that is, becoming like God. This means that it is a process of personal growth in which we deepen our relationship with God the Father. It is a process of growing in holiness which takes place also through our relationships with others and within the context of the creation. We do not progress in this saving relationship with God apart from others or apart from the creation. Rather, it is in the midst of life and in the midst of our relationships with others that we respond to God's gift of salvation and grow ever closer to him as his daughters and sons.

Christ as our Model and Goal

This Beatitude also points to the fact that we are meant to

be authentic persons who live seek to live a life of virtue following the example of Christ. For us, Christ is both the model and the goal of our human existence. The desire for God and the loving relationship which he offers inevitably involves a desire "to lead a life worthy of the calling" to which we have been called (Ephesians 4:1).

The actions and teachings of the Lord provide us with much valuable guidance on the identity and the style of life of a faithful Christian. Throughout our reflection on the Beatitudes, we see that Jesus identifies and honors characteristics of his faithful followers. In fact, he embodies the Beatitudes in his own life. In his relationship with God the Father, Jesus is poor in spirit and meek. He bears witness to the righteousness of God and expresses this in his dealings with others. While declaring the love of the Father, Jesus is merciful and mourns over the sins of others. While criticizing the hypocrisy of religious leaders, he is pure in heart and a maker of peace. Because of his love for the poor, the outcasts, the sinners, and the so-called "impure," he himself is persecuted. His love for the Father was intimately connected to his love for others, even those who rejected him and crucified him.

The Lord certainly did not provide his disciples with a book of rules and regulations which could be applied to every situation. This was not his intention. Rather, he came among proclaiming the Kingdom of God, and declaring God's love and mercy. His teachings, such a those in the Beatitudes, highlight the characteristics of those who live their lives in loving relationship with God and with others in the midst of the creation. His emphasis is upon those who have acknowledged the reign of God, and who are living as God's daughters and sons. And, of course, he offers his own example for us of a life which not only honors God and which cares for well-being of others but also proclaims the ultimate victory of God over all evil.

There is an intimate relationship between Christ and his life, and our effort to live a Christ-like life. Using marvelous images, Saint Ambrose of Milan speaks of the centrality of Christ when he says to us:

> In Christ we have everything.
> If you want to heal your wounds, he is the doctor.
> If you are burning with fever, he is the fountain.
> If you are in need of help, he is the strength.
> If you are in dread of death, he is life.
> If you are fleeing darkness, he is light.
> If you are hungry, he is food.
> O taste and see that the Lord is good.
> Happy are those who take refuge in him.[4]

The Struggle of Spiritual Growth

The relationship between Christ our Lord and each of us is deepened only through struggle. It is a struggle not because the Lord himself seeks to make the relationship trying or difficult. On the contrary, it is the greatest desire of the Lord that we share as fully as possible in his life. Rather, our relationship with Christ involves a struggle because we must do battle against those attitudes and forces which seek to keep us away from the Lord. There are obstacles which must be overcome as we grow closer to Christ.

The first obstacles which must be overcome is our own lack of desire and openness to God. Lack of openness to God is often referred to as "hardness of heart" in the Scripture and Tradition of the Church. Being open, even a little bit, is an act of trust in God which can have a life changing effect. If we wish for this relationship to grow, we must first of all truly be open to the possibility of experiencing a deepening of the bond between ourselves and Christ. This act of trust serves as a kind of "wordless prayer" which invites God to enter our lives in deep ways, in ways perhaps unknown before.

Despite the difficulties which may be in our way, we must desire to be open to responding to his presence as did Zacchaeus in the village of Jericho. Zacchaeus did what was necessary in order to respond to the presence of the Lord. He overcame the obstacle which was before him in order to see Christ and experience his love.

Every relationship requires a constant investment of ourselves. We must make the effort to nurture the relationship if it is to grow and not stagnate. The relationship between husband and wife, between parent and child, and between one friend and another requires special acts of personal attentiveness which express our love. If the relationship is to grow, each person involved must express his or her fidelity through the appropriate words and deeds of love.

Such loving deeds and words serve to build trust, confidence, knowledge, and understanding which are some of the important ingredients of a healthy relationship. When the loving deeds and words are not present, the relationship becomes stagnant. Its stagnation can be directly attributed to the fact that at least one person was not faithful.

Conversely, when the deeds and words of love are present, the relationship can flourish. It truly can become a blessing which enriches the lives of all involved in it.

The same principle applies to our relationship with God. As with our human relationships, our relationship with God requires that we actively seek to enhance our bond of love with him. When we are attentive to the relationship, it has the possibility for growth. The lack of attention on our part, however, can greatly harm our relationship with the Lord.

Let us remember that our Heavenly Father is always faithful. Even when we neglect him, he does not forget about us. He never abandons us and gives us up for lost. He is constantly offering his love. Christ, the Risen Lord, is ever present within the context of the responsibilities and relationships of our daily life. He always stands before us saying: "Come to me, all who labor and are heavy laden, and I will give you rest. Take my yoke upon you and learn from me; for I am gentle and lowly in heart, and you will find rest for your soul. For my yoke is easy, and my burden is light" (Matthew 11:28-30). The Lord never abandons us.

But…, we do not always respond to his presence. He calls to each of us daily but we frequently find ourselves not responding. Whether through our own inertia, pride, or ignorance, we do not always respond to him in a faithful manner which is honest and consistent.

Yes, when difficulties arise in our life, we may remember to "say a prayer" or to "go to church." But, when there are no apparent problems in our life, we often neglect our relationship with the Lord. We do not always take the time to nurture the relationship through prayer, through receiving Holy Communion, through reading the Scripture, and through doing acts of charity in his name. The special bond between him and us solemnly proclaimed at the time of our baptism often is forgotten.

If this is the way that we treat our relationship with the Lord, then, it should not be surprising that we can easily reach a point where we fail to experience his presence, or accept his mercy, or appreciate his unfailing love. At these times, we may feel that the Lord is absent or that he has abandoned us or that he does not care about us.

The Lord, however, has not abandoned us. We have in fact

abandoned the Lord. We have failed to hunger and thirst for him and his righteousness. And because of this, we have distanced ourselves from the Lord. We have absented ourselves from him. We have created a barrier between him and ourselves.

So, we have the obligation to seek the presence of the Lord in the midst of our daily responsibilities and obligations. Like Zacchaeus in Jericho, we must be ready and willing to overcome any obstacle which stands between the Lord and ourselves. This means that we must be willing to hear his words, to see his light, and to follow his example within the circumstances of our life in this world.

Saint Leo of Rome emphasizes the necessity of our cultivation of the desire for God when he says:

> The Lord says: 'Blessed are those who hunger and thirst for righteousness, for they shall be satisfied.' This hunger is not for bodily food; this thirst is not for earthly drink. These seek their satisfaction in the food of righteousness and the desire to be filled with the Lord himself.[5]

The second obstacle which we must overcome is an impoverished understanding of God. This may sound rather strange to some. But, the fact is that some of us have an understanding of God which does not correspond to the teachings about God which come from our Lord. Indeed, we may claim to be Christians, but some of us have a faulty understanding of "who" God is and "what" he does.

Some of us have a rather childish understanding of God. We have a tendency of attributing everything that happens in life to God. Yes, it is true that God is properly honored as the Creator. But, this does not mean that God is directly responsible for every human action or for every event which takes place in life.

Often, we fail to recognize both the reality of human freedom and the imperfect character of the material creation. As a consequence of this, we hold God responsible for everything which takes place in life including death and destruction. Far from believing in the God whom Jesus revealed to us, it seems that some of us have created a "god" who is capricious, vengeful, and wicked.

Likewise, some of us also believe in a "god" who does not care about each of us. Some of us have come to believe that we are not "good enough" for God. This belief may result from our own feelings of unworthiness as we noted earlier. Or, it may result from a sense of own personal failures and sins, Regardless of its source, however, some of us have come to believe that God does not care about us. Sadly, we may even come to believe this "god" is somehow seeking to do further damage to us.

Although Jesus teaches that the true God is a merciful Father who cares about each of us, some of us often believe that God is unable or unwilling to forgive us. We often believe that this "god" is plotting against us.

We have the responsibility to strive constantly to deepen our knowledge of the true God whom Jesus reveals to us. Certainly, the reading of the Scriptures and the writings of the great teachers of the Church can be helpful. The Scriptures and Tradition of the Church can point us in the proper direction and make us more receptive to the presence of the true and living God. Likewise, the relationship which we have with other believers, including the saints who have gone before us, can assist us in coming to know God better.

But, ultimately, we must realize that our personal relationship with the true God does not result directly from secondary sources. Rather, it comes primarily from personal experience nurtured in prayer, guided by the faith community, and centered upon Christ. We are meant not simply to know something "about God" but to truly know God through experience as our friend. By growing in our relationship with Christ, therefore, we have the opportunity to grow in our knowledge of the living God, to eliminate all our false perceptions of God and to experience in a deeply personal way the living God who is the source of life and holiness.

The third obstacle which we must overcome is the discouragement which may come from others. Devotion to the Lord and the firm desire to abide by his teachings will naturally have a positive affect upon the way which we lead our life. The values and perspectives of the Christian life as expressed in the Beatitudes are frequently quite different from the values of those who do not accept Christ as the Lord. In every aspect of life, the values and behavior of the believer will reflect the teachings of the Lord. As a consequence of this, we may find ourselves living our life in a manner which is quite different from the lives of some of our relatives, friends, and neighbors.

Our determination to live a Christian way of life, however, may not always be well received by others. Our life as a follower of Christ should be more loving of others, more understanding of others and more forgiving of others. It is a life from which we seek to remove all forms of false pride and arrogance which can hinder our relationship with others. Nonetheless, relatives and friends who have not consciously chosen to follow the Lord may become critical of our values and our behavior.

Our acceptance of Christ as our Lord and our determination to abide by his Gospel mean that we may become the target of criticism and unkind remarks from others. Either consciously or unconsciously, others may seek to discourage us from following Christ and living our lives according to his teachings. This discouragement can be very painful, especially when it comes from those who are close to us. It can be so painful, in fact, that it can even make us question the commitment which we have made.

So, our challenge is to maintain our commitment to the Lord and his teachings even in the face of discouragement which may come from others. Although we can pray that those who falsely criticize us or even hurt us, we are not in a position to change their views. They have to change themselves.

Bound Together in Christ

There are many obstacles to be faced as we grow in our relationship with God. Yet, we are not meant to face these and any other obstacles alone. It is especially at times when we encounter obstacles to our relationship with the Lord that we can appreciate the value of being part of the believing community of faith which is the Church.

At the time of our baptism, we not only became publicly united to Christ but also we became united with others who are part of the Church. We are members of the Body of Christ which is the community of believers which he established (1 Corinthians 12:12). We have fellow Christians to whom we can turn for support and encouragement. There is an ancient adage which says: "A solitary Christian is no Christian." This means that the very definition of Christian implies not only a relationship with Christ but also a relationship with others who are also faithful followers of Christ.

We can always seek out the support and guidance of fellow believer who understand the difficulties which we are encountering. The support which we receive from fellow believers, and especially our spiritual director, makes it easier for us to bear the subtle, and sometimes not so subtle, rejection of those who do not appreciate our commitment to the Lord. We can share our burdens with our fellow believers and we can gain strength from their support.

The Witness of the Saints

We also have the examples of those faithful women and men in every age and place who have been persons of pure heart and who have followed the Lord within the circumstances of their life in this world. Many of these persons are especially honored in a public way by the Church as "saints" because of their distinctive service to the Lord. Now, in the life to come, the saints are closer to God and pray for our progression in holiness. They are like a "cloud of witnesses" who surround us (Hebrews 12:1).

The saints are not to be seen as superhuman or as persons who lived an "easy" life in this world. Rather, they are human persons like us who lived in this world and who experienced many of the same challenges and difficulties, opportunities and joys that we also experience. Some of them were raised in faithful families. Others had the reputation of being sinners before their conversion to Christ and his Gospel. Some followed Christ from their youth. Others found him in their later years. Some were blessed with material wealth. Others were poor. What they all have in common is their devotion to the Lord. They sought to be faithful followers of Christ and to live their lives consciously as friends and servants of God. It was within the context of their life in this world that they matured in their relationship with God and progressed in holiness.

The example of the saints, therefore, can be very significant for us. By looking at their lives, we see that our Lord can be followed in a wide variety of circumstances and situations. Each saint in his or her own distinctive way has stood before God with integrity and has fulfilled the Gospel. Each has been a herald of the Father, a disciple of Christ, and a person filled with the Holy Spirit. In their progression in holiness in this world, the Saints did not loose those personal characteristics that made them unique. Rather, they responded in their particular situation to the call of the Lord and were open to the gifts of the Sprit.

Every Christian is called to be "holy," that is, to be a person who remembers God and is living in communion with God. Such a person is open to being a vehicle of God's grace and a faithful herald of God's presence in this world. This means that every Christian is called to be a "saint." Each Christian is called to be person through whom God works to bring about the salvation of the entire world.

Because of Christ, we are united with the Saints of every place and time in history through the fellowship of the Church. They are our brothers and sisters in the faith who now share in the joy of the heavenly Kingdom. We can learn from their example. And, we can also ask for their prayers. Because of their love for us, they pray to the Lord that we too may be faithful followers and inherit the Kingdom together with them.

The Blessing of Satisfaction

Our Lord Jesus Christ declares in the fourth Beatitude that those who hunger and thirst for righteousness will be satisfied.

The satisfaction about which the Lord speaks is ultimately nothing less than the experience of living our life in fellowship with God. Our hunger and thirst for that which is true and correct finds fulfillment in God himself. As the Lord says: "I will give water from the well of life free to anybody who is thirsty" (Revelations 21:6). The longing of our heart finds its ultimate goal to be God. The living God satisfies us with himself.

Our movement toward God, who is our true satisfaction, is a journey which begins at the very moment we are conceived and continues into eternity. It is a journey in which we are ever more perfected in love by being associated with the source of love. Our association with God is not one which destroys our unique identity. In our fellowship with God – the Father, the Son and the Holy Spirit – we always maintain our unique identity. It is an association in which our true identity is revealed and enriched. We come to know that we are a children of the Father, friends of Christ, and bearers of the Spirit.

Unlike sin which has the ability to distort our identity, the love of God restores and enriches our identity as we grow daily in our union with him. God has created each of us as a unique person. We are not meant to become an autonomous individual separated from God and his love. Rather, we have been created to experience the fullness of life in his love. Authentic human life consists of knowing, loving, and serving God in the midst of our daily responsibilities and relationships. It is for this reason that our Lord tells us that he has come so that we may have life in abundance (John 10:10).

Our Lord teaches us in the fourth Beatitude that those who hunger and thirst for righteousness will be satisfied. The satisfaction about which the Lord speaks is nothing less than God himself. The genuine efforts which we make to know, to love, and to serve God will bear fruit. We shall meet him as our friend. We shall be happy in the Lord.

From Our Christian Heritage

We do not have to toil and sweat to achieve our own perfection, nor are money and influence needed to obtain the gift of the Holy Spirit. It is freely given by God, always available for us to use. Just as the sun shines and the day brings light, the stream irrigates the soil and rain waters the earth, so the heavenly Spirit pours himself into us. Once we have lifted our eyes to heaven and acknowledged our creator, once we have been raised above the earth and rescued from slavery to this world, then we begin to be truly that new creation we believe ourselves to be.

We have received the seal of the Spirit. Our task now is to preserve the integrity of what we have received by living a truly Christian life. We must give our time to prayer and the study of scripture, now speaking to God, now listening to his word to us, and letting his teaching mold us. He has enriched us with a treasure no one can take away; we have eaten and drunk at his heavenly banquet, and we can never again know the pinch of poverty. Magnificent palaces are as nothing compared with the glory of our own soul which has become the Lord's temple with the Holy Spirit dwelling in it.

St. Cyprian of Carthage[6]

Prayer

Lord Jesus Christ, our God! Flood our souls with the radiant light of your wisdom, that we may serve you with renewed purity and integrity. Sunrise marks the time for us to begin our labors, but we implore you, master, to prepare in our souls a place for the day that never ends. Grant us a share in your risen life, let nothing distract us from the delights you offer, and by our tireless zeal for you, mark us by the sign of that day of yours that is not measured by the sun.

For you are, indeed, our God and we give you glory, together with your eternal Father and your all-holy, good, and life-giving Spirit: now and forever, and unto ages of ages. Amen.

Chapter Five

Blessed Are the Merciful
For They Shall Obtain Mercy

One day Jesus was teaching in the courtyard of the Temple in Jerusalem. While he was there, the Pharisees brought before him a woman who had been caught committing adultery (John 8:1-11). Priding themselves upon being the strict interpreters of the Law of Moses, the Pharisees declared that the woman deserved to be put to death. After all, they told Jesus, this is exactly what was taught in the Mosaic Law. And, indeed, they were correct. The ancient punishment for adultery was death. According to the laws which had been passed down to the Israelites from the time of Moses, adultery was a capital offense. The punishment was execution by stoning (Ezekiel 16:37ff).

Clearly, the intent of the Pharisees was to present Jesus with a "test case." They wanted to see whether or not Jesus would abide by the strict interpretation of the ancient law. Already Jesus and the Pharisees had come into conflict on a number of occasions with regard to the application of the law. Always troubled by the responses of the Lord, the Pharisees were preparing their own case against Jesus and his teaching. They would seek to show that Jesus could not possibly be the promised Messiah because of his apparent disregard for the ancient religious laws.

Jesus perceived the true intention of the Pharisees. The Lord knew that they wanted him to disregard publicly the stated punishment for adultery. Using the woman as their pawn, the

Pharisees were ready for a full fledged debate with Jesus about the correct interpretation of the law and its application.

With this in mind, Jesus used the opportunity to teach in a dramatic manner the meaning of mercy. Looking at the crowd, Jesus saw that each of those gathered were ready to stone the women to death. But, the Lord surprised them all. Rather than entering into a discussion with the Pharisees, he insisted the person who was without sin to come forward and cast the first stone at the woman. Of course, no one was able to do so. Each was ready to execute the woman. But, the Pharisees also knew in their deepest heart that they had also sinned and that they likewise were liable to punishment. So, one by one, they went away and left the woman with Jesus.

When Jesus was alone with the woman, the Lord declared that he would not condemn her. With words filled with compassion, Jesus said to her: "Go your way and do not sin again" (John 8:11).

Jesus bore witness to the mercy of God the Father with these simple but very powerful words. Jesus certainly did not condone the sinful action of the woman. He did not overlook the tragic consequence of sin. Indeed, in his confrontation with the Pharisees, he reminded all of their sins. Yet, the Lord boldly offered to the woman the mercy of God even though the ancient law dictated that she be stoned to death because of her sin. Through his words and deeds, Jesus declared that the woman, in spite of her sin, belonged to God and was of great value to him. Jesus forgave her and affirmed her true identity as a daughter of God, proclaiming to her the mercy of our heavenly Father.

The Gift of Mercy
Our Lord Jesus Christ says to us in the fifth Beatitude:

"Blessed are the merciful for they shall obtain mercy" (Matthew 5:7).

With these words, the Lord teaches us that his disciples are persons who are merciful because we recognize that God is merciful with us. In our dealings with others, we are meant to express the same mercy which God constantly shows to us. None of us is without sin, yet our heavenly Father is rich in mercy. He has created each of us and has called us to share in his life. He loves us as his daughters and sons. Even though we may forget him and fall into sin, he does not abandon us. He is "compassionate and gracious; he is slow to anger, rich in mercy" (Psalm 103 [102]:8).

Christ came into this world in order to embody the love, compassion, and mercy of God. He came to demonstrate both through his words and his deeds that God cares about each of us. Each of us is of supreme value to him. None of us is without ultimate value. The Good News is that God loves each of us and, because of this, Christ has come in order to restore us to fellowship with the Father. The Lord has come as the Way so that he may be our Truth and our Life (John 14:6).

From the time of Abraham, God revealed himself to the people of ancient Israel as the God of mercy who called all to share in his life. The ancient Israelites were invested with the mission of proclaiming this truth in a world where most people did not believe in the one true God. Yet, in spite of their vocation, there were times when the ancient Israelites themselves did not take seriously the fact that God was merciful. Since they did not fully understand the ways of God, often the ancient Israelites interpreted events to be a sign of divine vengeance and retribution.

Today, as we read parts of the Old Testament, it appears to us as though the ancient Israelites were not able always to comprehend that the Lord was the God of mercy who forgave transgression and sin (Exodus 34:7). They were not always able to understand that God was faithful even though they were often faithless. (Psalm 106 (105):7) Indeed, it appears that the ancient Israelites were sometimes troubled by the ability of God to accept the unworthy and to receive in love the sinners.

Because of the coming of Christ, we have gained a deeper insight into the merciful nature of God and the manner in which he deals with us. As the incarnate Son of God, Jesus has provided us with an understanding of God which is far richer and deeper than that which the ancient Israelites possessed. The one true God has not changed. But, we have been enriched with greater insight into his actions because of Christ. The fullness of God's revelation is expressed through the words and deeds of Christ. As the Epistle to the Hebrews says: "In many and various ways God spoke of old to our fathers by the prophets; but in these last days, he has spoken to us by a Son whom he appointed the heir of all things, through whom he also created the world" (Hebrews 1:1-2).

The affirmation that God is loving, merciful, and compassionate is at the very heart of the teaching and ministry of our Lord. Although we are not worthy of the compassion of God, Christ came into this world in order to restore us to fellowship with the Father (Ephesians 2:4). The Lord came to teach us that God is our Father and that he could not abandon us to the power of sin and death (Romans 8:32).

Rather, as the God of love (1 John 4:8), he has come into our midst in the person of Christ to demonstrate his unselfish and unconditional love for us (John 3:16). Although we are sinners, God in his mercy has saved us from the power of sin and gifted us with our knowledge of him through Christ (1 Timothy 1:15, 2:4). As the incarnate Son of God who knows our weakness,

Christ has also taught us how to respond through the Spirit to the mercy and love of the Father which come to us as a gift.

Speaking both of the profound love of God and the dignity of the human person, Saint Peter Chrysologus of Ravenna powerfully reminds us of all that God has done for us when he says:

> Why, people, you who are so precious to God, are you so worthless in your own eyes? Why render yourself such dishonor when you are honored by him? He made you in his image that you might in your person make the invisible Creator present on earth. He has made you his envoy so that the vast expanse of the earth might have the Lord's representative. Then, in his mercy, God assumed what he made in you. He wanted now to be truly manifest in you just as he had wished to be revealed in humankind as in an image... The fact that the Creator is in his creature and that God is in the flesh brings dignity to you without dishonor to him who made you.[1]

Throughout his ministry, our Lord constantly affirmed the mercy which God has for us and the fundamental dignity of every person created in the "image and likeness" of God (Genesis 1:26). We see this expressed especially in the way which Jesus treated others. The Lord was a friend of the sinner. He associated with the poor and the disabled. He treated women with respect. He did not turn away children. He honored the elderly. Although the Pharisees accused Jesus of eating with sinners and outcasts, time and again the Lord used the event of a meal shared with those in need to celebrate the mercy and forgiveness of the Father for all.

The Forgiving Father

The Lord taught about the mercy of God the Father and the dignity of the human person in many of his parables. Certainly, the parable of the Prodigal Son is one of the most important stories through which Jesus taught about God's faithful and compassionate love (Luke 15:11-32).

The young man in the story asked his father for his rightful inheritance. After receiving it, the young son left home for a distant land far from his father. There, he recklessly spent all of his inheritance and found himself without anything. Desperately needing to make a living, he found a job feeding pigs. One day, however, the young man came to his senses and recognized the folly of his ways. He resolved to return home and to seek the forgiveness of his father.

Even before he reached the door to his house, his father ran to greet him and to welcome the prodigal son home. A great banquet was prepared by the father to celebrate the return of his younger son. The compassionate father said to the servant: "Bring quickly the best robe and put it on him and put a ring on his hand and shoes on his feet; and bring the fatted calf and kill it, and let us eat and make merry; for this my son was dead, and is alive again; he was lost and was found" (Luke 15:24). The father showed no sign of vengeance or retribution. On the contrary, his mercy was overwhelming.

The story of the Prodigal Son is frequently remembered when we reflect upon our need for repentance. Like the son in the story, we sometimes find ourselves alienated from God because of our sins. We need to recognize the folly of our ways and return home to the love of God. We need to turn about and return to the house of our heavenly Father.

While not neglecting the important emphasis of the story upon repentance, we should not forget that the parable is also designed to teach us about the mercy of God. Indeed, it has been suggested that the story might better be called the "Parable of the Father's Love."

When Jesus told this story, he wanted to teach us that the compassionate action of the father in the parable is reflective of the way in which God treats us. We are the sons and daughters of the heavenly Father. Although we may turn away from him, God never abandons us. He is a merciful Father who patiently waits for us to return to his fellowship. Like the father in the story, God is always ready to welcome us back. His mercy is offered according to our need and not according to what we deserve.

Many of us do not believe that God is rich in mercy and full of compassion (James 5:11). While we believe that God exists, the difficulty which many of us have is to believe that God truly loves us in spite of our sins. Some of us have acquired a distorted understanding of God which does not reflect the teachings of Christ. Some of us have come to believe in a God of vengeance and retribution. Some of us have come to believe that God does not care about us. We have come to feel that God could not possibly love us. When we examine our sinful ways, it is difficult for us to believe that God is merciful, that he is always our loving Father.

Jesus reveals to us that God is our loving Father who is always merciful. Because of this, God does not condemn us when we sin (John 5:14). He does not abandon us even though we alienate ourselves from him through our sin. While not condoning our sins, he is faithful (1 John 1:9). He never forgets that we are his sons and daughters. He never disowns us or leaves us to be orphans. Like the father in the parable, our heavenly Father loves each of us and is always ready to receive us back into his family.

Reminding us of the mercy of God, Saint John Chrysostom tells us:

> Not only is it a wonderful thing that he forgives our sins, but also that he neither uncovers them nor does he make them stand forth clearly revealed. Nor does he force us to come forward and publicly proclaim our misdeeds, but he bids us to make our defense to him alone and to acknowledge our sins to him... God forgives our sins and does not force us to make a parade of them in the presence of others. He seeks one thing only: that the person who benefits by the forgiveness may learn the greatness of the gift.[2]

For us to appreciate the meaning of the fifth Beatitude, not only must we recognize that God is merciful but also we must recognize that we are in need of the mercy of God. We must come to appreciate the "greatness of the gift" which the Lord freely grants to us.

We have been called to live a life free from sin. As the Lord has said, we must strive to be whole and complete persons (Matthew 5:48). This means quite simply that we strive to do the good in all things. It means that we strive to live in a manner which befits the sons and daughters of God. As Saint Paul reminds us, we are meant to live a life worthy of our calling "with all lowliness and meekness, with patience, forbearing one another in love, eager to maintain the unity of the Spirit in the bond of peace" (Ephesians 4:2). As followers of Christ, we are called to live in a distinctive manner through which we love God and love others as we love ourselves.

While we affirm that God is our Father and that we are his children, the fact remains, however, that we do not always live our lives in his presence. We do not always seek his will. We do not always live up to our fundamental vocation of being his sons and daughters. Every form of sin distorts our relationship with God and with others. Every form of sin distorts our identity as his daughters and sons.

So, we must be willing to honestly recognize our sin. This involves a clear recognition that there have been times when we have not lived up to our vocation to live as the sons and daughters of God. There have been times when we have done what we should not have done or failed to do what we should have done. There have been times when we have spoken words which should not have been said and failed to speak when we should have. While we are truly the sons and daughters of God, "all of us have sinned and fallen short of the glory of God" (Romans 3:26). As a consequence of this fact, we always stand in need of the mercy of God.

We are the unworthy recipients of his mercy although we justly deserve the harsh judgment of God because of our sin. Because of his love for us, God forgoes judgment and offers us his forgiveness. Like the prodigal son, we have squandered the inheritance which has been given to us. We are not worthy to return to our father's house. Like the woman caught in adultery, we stand before God as a sinner. We are not even worthy to enter into his presence.

Despite our sins, however, God our heavenly Father loves us as his unique sons and daughters. He receives us as his children. In showering us with his compassion, God never forgets that we are his. While our sins would condemn us, we are gifted with his mercy.

Authentic growth in our relationship with God involves both a deepened awareness of the danger of sin and a deepened awareness of the mercy of God. As Saint John has reminded us, none of us is without sin (1 John 1:10). None of us is in a position where we can "pick up the first stone" and cast it in the direction of another sinner. Yet, at the same time, no follower of Christ can deny the fact of the mercy of God. Indeed, if God remembered our sins, none of us would be able to stand in his presence (Psalm 130:3). God our Father is merciful (Luke 6:35). With this truth in mind, we are called to recognize his generous mercy and to bear witness to his compassion in our life.

Being Merciful

Our Lord has come not only to teach us about God but also to teach us about ourselves. As we have already said, Christ has revealed to us that God the Father is merciful. In like manner, the Lord also teaches us that we are called to be merciful. Jesus says to us: "Be merciful as your heavenly Father is merciful" (Luke 6:36). In this forceful admonition, our Lord is telling us that our behavior towards others should reflect the way which God treats us. As the persons who are deeply conscious of the mercy of God, we are also meant to be merciful towards others.

When we freely choose to forego revenge and to offer another person mercy, we are bearing witness through our own words and deeds to the mercy which we have received from God. Having been gifted with the mercy of God, we are meant to share that mercy with others. Being merciful is a fundamental characteristic of our life as followers of Christ.

Throughout our study of the Beatitudes, we have seen that the way which we approach God cannot be separated from the way we treat others. There is a clear connection between our love for God and our love for others. We cannot claim to love God and not behave in a loving manner toward others. We cannot claim to love the God of mercy and not be willing to behave in a merciful manner toward others. So close is this relationship that Saint Anthony says: "Our life and our death is with our neighbor. If we gain our brother, we have gained God. But if we scandalize our brother, we have sinned against Christ."[3]

Our compassionate love for others is meant to express itself in very concrete ways. Mercy manifests itself not only in forgiveness but also in offering others what they need. We show mercy for the hungry by providing food, for the thirsty by providing drink, for the stranger by providing hospitality, for the naked by providing clothing, for the sick by caring for them, and for those in prison by visiting them (Matthew 25:31-36). As Saint Gregory of Nyssa says: Mercy "is the parent of kindness and the pledge of love, it is the bond of all loving disposition."[4]

The parable of the Last Judgment (Matthew 25:31-46) has served as the background for the two lists of Christian responsibilities known as "The Spiritual Works of Mercy" and "The Physical Works of Mercy." While the responsibilities noted are not meant to exhaust all the possibilities of service to others, they do remind us of the many ways in which we are called to express mercy.

The Spiritual Works of Mercy are:
> To admonish sinners
> To instruct the ignorant
> To council the doubtful
> To comfort the sorrowful
> To suffer wrongs patiently
> To forgive injuries
> To pray for the living and the dead.

The Physical Works of Mercy are:
> To feed the hungry
> To give drink to the thirsty

To cloth the naked
To shelter the homeless
To visit the imprisoned
To care for the sick
To bury the dead

We know that we are frequently tempted to demonstrate our love only for those who are in positions of power and prestige. We are sometimes prone to do good only for those who can do something for us in return. We are sometimes prone to "follow the crowd" and to behave in ways which will gain approval in the eyes of others.

As followers of the Lord, however, we need to remember that Christ identified himself with the needy. He was always compassionate to those who, some would claim, did not appear to "deserve" compassion. In order to bear witness to the love of God for those in need, the Lord frequently ignored the conventional customs and practices of his day.

When confronted with those who spoke about religious rules and regulations, the Lord said: "The Sabbath was made for humankind, not humankind for the Sabbath" (Mark 2:27). With these words, the Lord affirmed that religious rules are not ends in themselves. They are meant to serve us in our progression toward God and not become impediments. By no means were religious rules meant to diminish the supreme dignity of the human person. The Lord affirmed that human persons were of greatest importance.

Indeed, it was because of this that the Lord was frequently accused of "irreligious" behavior by members of the religious establishment. These persons claimed to be faithful adherents to the traditional religious laws, but in reality their hearts were hardened to the presence of God. They claimed to have great respect for the laws but treated some persons with contempt. The harshest criticism which Jesus expressed was to those who claimed to be the leaders of religion but whose lives were filled with pride, self-righteousness, and hypocrisy (Matthew 23:1-37).

Mercy is truly a gift of compassionate love freely offered to another person in imitation of the way in which God treats us. When we behave in a merciful way towards others we are expressing our love for one another by rejecting retribution and by offering forgiveness. Mercy means that we choose not to act in an evil way toward another who has offended us. Mercy means that we do not think evil of another. Mercy means that we pray for the well-being of both those who love us and those who hate us. Mercy means that we seek to do good towards another who is in need.

The follower of Christ is called by the Lord to be merciful towards others. To be merciful towards others, however, does not mean that we condone sin or evil. Mercy is a gift of compassionate love offered to a person. It is not the approval of what is truly sinful behavior. While we are called by the Lord to be merciful, we are also called to oppose all types of sinful behavior both in ourselves and in others. Indeed, we must be constantly vigilant to the danger of sinful behavior in ourselves, in others, and in groups of persons.

Pride, envy, lust and greed are sins which often lead to other sins. These sins may be the neglect of the less fortunate, the oppression of the weak and the discrimination of those who are different from us. Thus, while we are called to be merciful toward sinners, we are also obliged to oppose all forms of sinful behavior.

There is no doubt about the fact that it is not always easy for us to be merciful toward others. Most of us would agree in principle that it is good for us to be merciful as God is merciful to us. But, most of us have difficulty in applying this principle in daily situations.

It is very difficult, for example, to be merciful in the face of the sinful behavior of others. It is difficult to be merciful in the face of gossip, slander and the disregard for truth which can be expressed by others. It is difficult to be merciful towards those who hurt us or who hurt those whom we love. It is not always easy to follow the example of the Lord, who even forgave those who crucified him (Luke 23:34).

Our Lord did not say that our life of discipleship would be easy. He did not say that we would not have to make difficult decisions or to behave in a manner which was contrary to the expectations of some. No, he did not say that being a disciple of his would be easy. But, he did say that he would be with us (Matthew 28:20). He did say that the Spirit would guide us (John 16:13). These words of assurance may serve to remind us that the Lord himself will provide us with the resources to live our lives as his disciples. So, when we truly desire to be merciful in the midst of a difficult situation, he will provide us with the necessary strength to be merciful. Although we may face many difficulties, we know that ultimately "our help is in the name of the Lord" (Psalm 124:8).

We should also be aware of another important aspect of the giving of mercy to another. When we express our love in the gift of mercy, there is no guarantee that the other person will accept or honor our gift of mercy. Each person is free either to accept the mercy which we offer or to reject it. When mercy is freely offered and freely accepted there is joy. However, when mercy is freely offered but not accepted there is sorrow. Yet, whether or not our gift of mercy is accepted by another person, we have the obligation as followers of the Lord to be merciful towards others as our heavenly Father is merciful toward us.

As we grow in our appreciation of the mercy of God, so also the boundaries of our mercy increases. Our mercy moves beyond those whom we know to those whom we do not know, beyond the human world to the world of the animals, beyond what we see to that which we do not see.

This is the truth reflected in the following observation by Saint Isaac the Syrian when he says:

> And what is a merciful heart? The burning of the heart on account of all creation, on account of people and birds and animals and demons, and for every created being. Because of their remembrance, the eyes fill with tears. Great and intense mercy grasps the heart and wings it out, for the person who is merciful is not able to bear or hear or see any harm, or the slightest sorrow taking place in the created world. This holds true on behalf of those who harm him. For these, the person offers prayers continually with tears for their protection and redemption. He does so even for the snakes which crawl upon the ground. All of this the person does out of his great mercy, which moves in his heart without measure in the likeness of God.[5]

As we continue to meditate upon the effects of mercy we find something else happening as well. We find that our own personal efforts of mercy somehow progressively change us. It is impossible to remain the same if we continue to cultivate a merciful heart. This positive change is a consequence of living mercifully. The mercy we send off somehow "bounces back" in other ways. Through the exercise of mercy, we become more fully the sons and daughters of God.

The Blessing of Mercy

Our Lord Jesus Christ declares in the fifth Beatitude that those who are merciful shall obtain mercy.

The love which God has for each of us is unconditional. He cares for each of us as his son or daughter. As a loving Father, he is rich in mercy. He never forgets us or abandons us even though we may fall into sin. God's love is not contingent upon our love for him. His mercy is not dependent upon our ability to be merciful. While we may sin and neglect our relationship with him, God is "faithful and just, and will forgive our sins and cleanse us from all unrighteousness" (1 John 1:9).

However, each of us must respond to God and his love. Since we are blessed with the gift of free will, God does not impose himself upon us. He does not force us to accept his love. He does not compel us to experience his mercy. Whether we respond or not depends upon our disposition. God respects our freedom.

Our movement toward God involves living our lives as persons who imitate the actions of God. As we have already said, God has revealed himself to be a loving Father who is compassionate and filled with mercy for his daughters and sons. Those who have chosen to seek God in this life know that our actions are meant to mirror the actions of God. We are called to love one another because he first loved us. We are called to forgive because he has first forgiven us. We are called to be merciful because he was first merciful toward us.

As we grow in our ability to love in an unselfish way, we become more sensitive to God's love for us. As we deepen our ability to forgive, we become more conscious of God's forgiveness of our sins. As we cultivate our ability to be merciful, we become more receptive to God's mercy. Those who have obtained the mercy of God are those who recognize their need for divine forgiveness and who offer mercy to others. These are the disciples of the Lord who have realized that the Father is a God of mercy who calls us to be merciful.

Through imitating the actions of God, we come to know him better and are drawn more closely to him.

Our Lord teaches us in the fifth Beatitude that those who are merciful toward others follow the example of God. Our heavenly Father is rich in mercy and compassion. Those of us who are merciful toward others are able to experience the compassion which God has for us. We shall be happy in the Lord.

From Our Christian Heritage

So if I have convinced you of anything, O servants of Christ, who are my brothers and fellow heirs, let us while there is still time visit Christ in his sickness, let us have a care for Christ in his sickness, let us give to Christ to eat, let us clothe Christ in his nakedness, let us do honor to Christ, and not only at table as some do, not only with precious oil as Mary did, not only at his tomb as Joseph of Arimathea did, he who was a half follower of Christ, not only showing him honor with gold, frankincense and myrrh, as the Magi did… but let us honor him because the Lord of all will have mercy and not sacrifice, and goodness of heart above thousands of fat lambs. Let us give him this honor in his poor, in those who lie on the ground before us this day, so that when we leave this world they may receive us into the eternal dwelling place, in Jesus Christ our Lord, to whom be glory now and forever, and unto ages of ages. Amen.

Saint Gregory the Theologian[6]

Prayer

Hear us, Lord, and have mercy on us, for you are merciful! Enable us to cling to the ways of your law, in your footsteps, lest our feet stumble. Teach us your ways, that we may walk in your truth. Let our prayer reach you. Attend to our plea, for we have had our fill of trouble and our life is on the brink of the grave. Be mindful of us O Lord, when you show favor to your people; take note of us when you save them.

For you are full of mercy and compassion, O God, and we give you glory, Father, Son, and Holy Spirit: now and forever, and unto ages of ages. Amen.

Chapter Six

Blessed Are the Pure in Heart
For They Shall See God

While traveling to Jerusalem, our Lord and his disciples passed through the town of Jericho. It was probably the last visit of the Lord to this village located about ten miles northeast of the capital. It was the same village in which Zacchaeus lived. Since the Lord had been preaching for about three years, many people of the area had heard about Jesus and wanted to get near him. Sitting along the road where Jesus was walking was a man named Bartimaeus who was a blind beggar.

When Bartimaeus heard that it was Jesus who was passing through, he began to call out saying: "Jesus, Son of David, have mercy upon me" (Mark 10:47). Perhaps the blind man had heard the Lord teaching and now he sought to get close to Christ. But, the bold call of Bartimaeus was not simply a call for help. Bartimaeus could have called to anyone in the crowd if he only wanted physical assistance. His words were a profession of faith! Although he could not see, it seems that Bartimaeus truly sought the Lord with all his heart.

When people in the crowd heard the call of the blind beggar, they rebuked him. Most probably with anger and scorn in their voice, they told Bartimaeus to be silent. In those days, many people believed that physical disabilities were a punishment from God. Many also believed that persons with disabilities were somehow "unclean" and undeserving of attention. So, many people in the crowd probably felt that Jesus would have nothing to do with a blind beggar.

Despite their discouragement, however, Bartimaeus refused to be silent. He called out even more strongly saying: "Jesus, Son of David, have mercy on me!" (Mark 10:48). Bartimaeus refused to be discouraged by those around him. His intention was pure and genuine. Although he could not see the Lord with his eyes, Bartimaeus' heart was centered upon Jesus.

Jesus heard the call of Bartimaeus. Of all the people in the crowd that day, it was the voice of the blind beggar, which caught his attention. Perhaps the Lord knew that the person who called out was a man of integrity and faith who truly sought God with all his heart. Jesus stopped and told his disciples to call the man. Finding the blind beggar sitting at the side of the road, they said to Bartimaeus: "Take heart, rise, he is calling you" (Mark 10:49). The words of the disciples must have been truly "good news" for Bartimaeus. Immediately, the blind beggar threw off the cloak which covered him, jumped to his feet and made his way through the crowd with the help of the disciples.

When Bartimaeus came before the Lord, Jesus said to him: "What do you want me to do for you?" And the blind man said to him, "Master, let me receive my sight." And Jesus said to him, "Go your way your faith has made you well" (Mark 11:51-52). At that very moment, Bartimaeus was able to see and he began to follow Christ.

We know nothing more of Bartimaeus. Yet, the story of his encounter with Christ reveals to us a person of faith who sought the Lord with all his heart. Undaunted by the discouragement of the crowd, Bartimaeus was a person of conviction who came to "see" Christ and became a follower of the Lord.

Purity of Heart

Our Lord Jesus Christ says to us in the sixth Beatitude: "Blessed are the pure of heart for they shall see God" (Matthew 5:8).

With these words, the Lord teaches us that his disciples are persons who stand before God with integrity, honesty, and without pretense. The person who is "pure in heart" is one who is truly devoted to God and his service. It is a description of those persons "whose minds are not obsessed by idols, who do not swear deceitfully. They shall carry away a blessing from the Lord, a just reward from God their savior. Such are they who turn to the Eternal One, who seek out the presence of the God of Jacob" (Psalm 24 [23]:4-6).

As in the time of our Lord's life on earth, the word "heart" is often used today to refer not only to the organ within us but also to the entire person. Perhaps because it is the organ most essential for sustaining life, the "heart" has come to represent the very essence of a person.

We frequently use the word "heart" in various ways to describe the inner character of a person. When we speak of someone whose "heart is broken," for example, we are referring to a person whose feelings have been deeply hurt. And, by the same token, when we speak of doing something "wholeheartedly," we mean that the entire self is doing it without reservation. When a person is exceptionally generous, we say that he or she has a "heart of gold." And, when a person is lacking in the ability to love or to forgive, we say that he or she is "hardhearted."

These uses of the word "heart" have deep roots in the history of our language and frequently reflect scriptural insights. So, our use of the term "heart" to express the inner character of a person helps us to understand what our Lord meant when he spoke of the "pure of heart" in this beatitude. To be pure in heart is not simply to be a person of moral purity. Rather, the phrase points to a deeper reality. The one who is pure in heart is the person who, first of all, stands before God with honesty and without pretense. Purity of heart is a mature stance of awareness, receptivity and innocence in the presence of God.

The Parable of the Pharisee and the Tax Collector (Luke 18:9-14) is a story which provides us with a vivid picture of two men as they stand before God with two very different attitudes of the heart. The Lord tells us that both men went to the temple in order to pray. Both of these men offered their prayers to God. Yet, each man had a very different manner of approaching God. Each expressed a very different spiritual attitude.

The first man was a Pharisee. This meant that he was a member of group of men who comprised one of a number religious parties within Judaism at the time of our Lord. What distinguished the Pharisees from the other groups was chiefly their strict interpretation of the Mosaic Laws. They believed that the Mosaic Laws had to be strictly followed at all times without any regard for persons or circumstances.

There were some Pharisees who eventually came to accept Christ as the Messiah. There were many others, however, who opposed Christ and plotted against him (Matthew 12:14). Throughout his ministry, Jesus often criticized their self-righteousness and hypocrisy (Luke 11:37ff).

The second man was a tax collector. As we have already noted in our discussion of Zacchaeus, tax collectors were not generally held in high esteem at the time of our Lord. The tax collectors in Palestine were usually Jews who worked for the Roman government as civil servants. This is the reason that the tax collector is sometimes referred to as a "publican" in some translations of the New Testament. Many Jews, especially the

Pharisees, viewed the tax collector with contempt. Not only was the tax collector seen as being dishonest but also he was seen as an agent of a foreign government.

Despite the reputation which tax collectors had, however, Jesus had at least two of them as followers. Matthew the Apostle and Evangelist was called by the Lord from the tax collector's table (Matthew 9:9). And, as we mentioned earlier, Jesus went to the house of the tax collector Zacchaeus. Because of this, the Lord was accused by the Pharisees of being a friend of tax collectors and sinners (Luke 7:34).

In the parable, the Pharisee prayed in a manner which seems to reflect the characteristics which Christ criticized. The Pharisee said: "God, I thank you that I am not like other men, extortioners, unjust, adulterers, or even like this tax collector. I fast twice a week, I give tithes of all that I get." (Luke 18:11-12). In praying to God, the Pharisee expressed no contrition. On the contrary, he set himself above others and appeared to brag about his accomplishments. He approached God not with a contrite heart but rather with a heart filled with self-centered contempt for others.

The prayer of the tax collector was very different. Standing toward the rear of the temple, the tax collector beat his breast as an expression of contrition and said: "God be merciful to me a sinner." (Luke 18:13).

The words spoken by these two men reveal their inner attitude toward God. Despite the fact that the Pharisee apparently had not fallen into certain sins, he boastfully compared himself to the tax collector and expressed in his prayer a self-righteousness and prideful attitude before God. The tax collector, on the other hand, came into the presence of God in humility and with a contrite heart. There was no pretense in his voice. There was honesty in his word. He was a person of integrity.

In this powerful story, it is the tax collector who comes before God with integrity and true devotion. The tax collector is the one whose heart is pure even though he fully recognizes his sins. He does not approach God with arrogance or pride. On the contrary, he appears to come before God with a genuine understanding of himself and his condition. He seeks neither to fool himself nor to fool God. He stands before God with a pure heart. Indeed, this is exactly what the Lord implies when he concludes the story by saying: "I tell you this man went down to his house justified rather than the other; for everyone who exalts himself will be humbled, but he who humbles himself will be exalted" (Luke 18:14).

Placing God First

Because we are followers of Christ, we have the obligation to center our life upon God and his service. Our Lord reminds us of this obligation to seek God in all things when he says to us: "Seek first his Kingdom and his righteousness..." (Matthew 6:33). With these forceful words, Jesus is emphasizing the fact that our entire existence must first of all be oriented toward God. We are called to be "theocentric" persons whose daily existence is centered upon the reality of God.

God is our Father and the source of all life and holiness. To believe this means that no person or thing can be more important to us than he is. Our true devotion and our ultimate loyalty must always be to him. No person or thing in this life can replace his importance. We must be careful not replace the living God with an idol which detracts us from him and becomes more important to us. Rather, the living God must always be the most important subject of our concern and the very center of our existence.

All of our spiritual disciplines are meant to reoriented ourselves towards God and to disassociate ourselves from every type of sin. When we pray, fast, receive Holy Communion, and meditate upon the Scriptures, for example, we are engaged in a process "changing our hearts." We are opening our hearts up to the presence of the living God.

Our devotion to the Lord, however, cannot be expressed without reference to the various relationships, responsibilities of our life. We simply cannot know God, love God and serve God outside or apart from the context of life in this world.

This means that the followers of the Lord are not called by Christ to neglect our relationships with other human persons and our responsibilities in the society. We are not called to forget about our obligations within our homes or within the broader community. We are not called to diminish the importance of the loving relationships which we have with others. As persons who are called to be the "salt of the earth" and the "light of the world," we have an obligation to be faithful to the relationships and responsibilities which characterize our life (Matthew 5:13-14).

Placing God first in our life does not mean that we do not have other legitimate concerns. We do in fact have many legitimate concerns which deserve our care and attention. These concerns have to do with our own desires to mature in a manner which gives glory to God. These concerns also have to do with our relationships with others and with our responsibilities in the home and the society.

Recognizing the importance of our personal relationship with God does not mean that we fail to recognize the importance of the relationships which we have with others. Recognizing our obligations to God does not mean that we do not recognize the significance of the obligations which we have to others in our home, at work, in our local community or society at large.

To place God at the very center of our existence should properly mean that the reality of God and our relationship to him is meant to have a bearing upon every other aspect of our life. All of our relationships and responsibilities are meant to be reflective of our fundamental relationship with God. Every aspect of our life is meant to be transfigured by his presence in our life. We come to know God, love God and serve God within the context of the relationships and responsibilities of our daily life. And, it is these relationships and responsibilities that are meant to be illuminated by our devotion to God.

One of the most serious distortions of Christian spirituality is the one which views life as being divided into two major parts: one which is "religious"; and the other which is "non-religious."

There are some of us who believe that our relationship with God is unrelated to the other relationships and responsibilities of our life. For those of us who believe this, the religious part of our life is usually limited to the confines of Sunday morning. That is the time when we think of God, when we pray, and when we go to church. This religious segment of our life is neatly separated and detached from the rest of our life. Our Sunday morning "religious activities," such as they are, seem unrelated to the rest of the week. Our relationship with God, such as it is, seems to have little impact upon the values in our home or in our workplace. When asked about our faith, we may vigorously profess that we are followers of Christ. Yet, the sad fact remains that the Gospel of the Lord has not illuminated every aspect of our life.

Christ wants to be the Lord of all of our life. There can be no dichotomy or separation between our relationship with him and our relationship with others. Those who seek to be "pure in heart" are those who strive to know, to love, and to serve God in and through every aspect of our life.

Our life is meant to be wholly and completely open to the Lord's presence. Our values should properly reflect our faith convictions. This means that the manner in which we treat ourselves, other persons, the manner we treat other members of our family, the manner which we relate to our co-workers, the manner in which we behave as a citizens are meant to be profoundly affected by our relationship with Christ. For those of us who have accepted Christ as the Lord of our life, no aspect of our existence is beyond the boundary of the light of his Gospel.

Many early Christian teachers speak about the balance and interrelationship between our faith in God, our worship of God and our responsibilities to God expressed through our love for others. Our faith is expressed not only in our worship but also in our concerns for others. Likewise, our concern for others and the society in which we live must also be nurtured by our faith and sustained through our worship.

Our progress toward the God the Father through Christ is always a movement within the context of our life situation nurtured by the Spirit. The Risen Christ comes to us within the context of the relationships and responsibilities of our life in this world. So, our response to the presence of the Lord also must be within the fabric of our life in this world.

This is precisely the approach which Saint Paul has in mind when he says: "And whatever you do, in word or deed, do everything in the name of the Lord Jesus, giving thanks to God the Father through him" (Colossians 3:17).

Seeking the Lord in all things requires a constant effort on our part to cleanse our hearts from every form of deception which take us away from God. The Gospel of the Lord challenges us not only to live our life in fellowship with God but also to live a life worthy of our calling (Ephesians 4:1). This means that we concern ourselves daily with loving God, with deepening our knowledge of God, and with serving God. It is in this way that we gradually acquire the purity of heart.

As the sons and daughters of the Father, we are called to cleanse ourselves not only from of all forms of impurity but also from all forms of self-deception. This involves the rejection of every expression of pretense and false visions of self. This requires both the rejection of sin and the affirmation of an honest way of living which brings glory to God our Heavenly Father. In the words of the Psalms, we must constantly pray: "Let not my heart turn to wrong, to making excuses for sinning with the wicked" (Psalm 141 [140]:4. And, we must strive to live according to this prayer.

The persons in the Gospels whom Jesus challenged repeatedly were the Scribes and Pharisees. The Lord was critical of them chiefly because they pretended to be persons that they were not. The Scribes and Pharisees saw themselves as the principle teachers of the ancient Mosaic laws. Yet, many of them allowed a great gap to develop between what they taught and how they lived. Although they claimed to be teachers of religion, their hearts were hardened. They placed faithfulness to the Law above compassion for the "living icons" of God. They claimed to speak about the things of God, yet, they were unwilling to let God's light enter into their very beings.

Enjoying their status in the society, the Scribes and Pharisees treasured the "masks" which they created. They pretended to be people they really were not. They did not stand before God with humility but with pride. And, because of their pretense, the Lord referred to them as hypocrites and blind guides. The Lord said that the Pharisees were "like whitewashed tombs, which outwardly appear very beautiful, but within they are full of dead men's bones and all uncleanness" (Matthew 24:27).

Saint Gregory of Nyssa speaks of the importance of truly knowing ourselves when he says:

> Our greatest protection is self-knowledge, and the avoidance of the delusion that we are seeing ourselves when we are really looking at something else. This is what happens to those who do not examine themselves: What they see is strength, beauty, reputation, political power, great wealth, pomp, self-importance, bodily stature... and they think that this is what they are. Such persons make very poor guardians of themselves. Because of their absorption in something else, they overlook what is their own and leave it unguarded. How can a person protect what he does not know? The most secure protection for our treasure is to know ourselves: each one of us must know himself as he is so that he may not be unconsciously protecting something else other than himself.[1]

To be pure in heart requires that we actively seek to rid ourselves of all forms of pretense and deception. We must rid ourselves of the "masks" which depict us as persons whom we are not and conceal our true identifies. We must struggle to be the persons whom we truly are. Honestly recognizing our personal strengths and limitations, we must be willing to let the light of Christ enter into every aspect of our life.

Fellowship with Others

Each of us must follow the Lord in a manner which is deeply personal. All of us struggle in our own way to purify our heart and draw closer to our Lord. But, none of us is meant to follow Christ as a solitary disciple. Our Lord does not intend this. On the contrary, he intends that grow in our relationship with him through fellowship with others. We are not saved alone but we are saved in fellowship with others. There can be no such person as a solitary Christian. Through the activity of the Holy Spirit, we are "knit together in love" with all those other persons who are united with Christ (Colossians 2:2).

This means that each of us is meant to be a member of a particular community of faith which is known as a parish. It is within the life of this parish that believers are brought together for common worship, for common witness and service, as well as for fellowship in the name of the Lord. It is within this community of faith that our own faith is nurtured and guided. It is within this community of faith that we benefit from the witness of other believers. It is within this community of faith that we have the opportunity to aid others in their growth in Christ. Our relationship with Christ takes place in conjunction with the relationships we have with others who share our faith convictions and values.

Every Christian also benefits greatly from a personal relationship with a spiritual director. Throughout the course of Christian history, different names have been used to designate this special person to whom one goes for guidance in the faith. This person has been known as a spiritual father or mother, as an elder or a guide. In the early Church in Ireland, the spiritual director was known as the "soul friend." This ancient description reminds us vividly of the mutual relationship which we are meant to have with our spiritual director.

Many contemporary Christians often view the pastor of their parish as their "spiritual director." Looking at the vast history of the Church, however, we see that spiritual directors have not always been ordained members of the clergy nor have they always been men. Often in the past, it was a pious and highly respected monk or nun who was recognized as a "spiritual director." Today, we recognize that the "spiritual director" can be a gifted and mature person, either a man or a women, who is firmly rooted in the faith, and who has the distinct gift and ability to nurture others in the faith.

Growth in the Christian life is a joyful process but also one fraught with challenges and difficulties. Those who make a serious commitment to follow Christ are in great need of assistance from a more mature guide who can nurture us in the Christian journey. We can benefit greatly from the wisdom of another believer who is well aware of both the challenges and the difficulties of Christian life. Each of us can benefit in personal guidance in cultivating the spiritual disciplines such as prayer, fasting, and almsgiving.

Like a father or mother in the faith, this skilled person can nurture us as we mature in our Christian life. This person can help us to relate the teachings of the faith to the particular reality of our life. This is why Saint Basil advises us to find a person "who may serve you as a very sure guide in the activity of leading a holy life which you wish to undertake. Choose one who knows how to show souls of good will the straight road to God."[2]

Left to our limited experience, we are often prone to misunderstand the meaning of scriptural passages and to misinterpret the stirring in our heart. While God is certainly at work in our lives, we can easily mistake our own selfish desires for his activity. Much damage can be done by a Christian who thinks that he or she is obeying God but who in reality is being fooled and led away from God due to a lack of spiritual wisdom.

We simply cannot be our own guides in our journey toward our heavenly Father. We need to be not only a member of a community of faith. We also need a faithful and trusted guide who will point us in the proper direction, correct us when we need correction, and encourage us at all times.

The spiritual director has two important characteristics which enable him or her to undertake this special ministry. Firstly, the spiritual director is a person of discernment. As the fruit of his or her own faith development, the spiritual director is able to see into the heart of another and to provide insight into that person's life. The spiritual director does not impose his or her opinion. Rather, the director seeks to enable the other person to mature in his or her relationship with the Lord and with others.

Often the director sharing aspects of his or her own progress in the faith does this. The insights which the director offers are especially important not simply because they reflect his or her own struggle. They are important also because they reflect the great wisdom embodied in the spiritual tradition of the Church as well as an understanding of the various aspects of personal development.

Secondly, the spiritual director has the ability freely to love the other person in a manner which affirms that person's identity as a son or a daughter of God, which nurtures that person's spiritual gifts, and which encourages that person's service in Christ's name. In order to do this, the spiritual director is ready and willing to bear the burdens of the other person, to listen patiently to the other's concerns, and to pray for the other.

The Blessing of Seeing God

Our Lord Jesus Christ declares in the sixth Beatitude that those who are pure in heart shall see God.

Throughout our study of the Beatitudes, we have recognized that certain words or phrases must be understood within the wider context of the teachings of Christ as expressed in the scriptures and tradition of the Church. This is certainly true of the concept of "seeing" God.

We have gained an insight into the mystery of God because God has chosen to reveal himself to us. This divine revelation is centered upon the reality of Christ and his teachings. We have come to know something about the Triune God, ourselves, and the world in which we live because of God's self disclosure. At the same time, we also recognize that this revelation does not exhaust the mystery of God.

With this in mind, there are two concerns regarding our understanding of God which at first may seem contradictory but are in fact complementary in so far as we have some insight into the mystery of God.

On the one hand, there is a strong affirmation that God is beyond us as well as the material world. Although he is the Creator, he is not to be identified with the physical world. God is the Creator of heaven and earth. God is not a creature. He is beyond all materiality. As Jesus himself said: "God is spirit" (John 4:24). This means that God quite simply is not observable, he cannot be "seen" with the physical eye.

Having said this, there is another affirmation which must be as forcefully made. Following the teachings of our Lord, Christians also affirm that we are called by the Living God to enter into a deeply personal and intimate relationship with him. This relationship has its origin in God's own love for us. It is not a relationship which we can create or manipulate. We can, however, choose to respond in love to the God who first loves us and who has revealed himself to us.

Because of this fact, Jesus frequently used very powerful words to help us understand this deeply personal relationship which God offers to each of us. As we have said elsewhere, Jesus speaks, for example, of God as being "our Father." He refers to us as the "children" of God. He tells us that the Kingdom of heaven is "within us." And, likewise, he tells us that "the pure in heart shall see God."

When the Lord tells us that the pure in heart shall see God, he is emphasizing the fact that these persons are able, through God's grace, to have an intimate and deeply personal experience of God. Jesus does not mean that we shall "see" God with our physical eyes precisely because God cannot be seen. Reflecting the rich imagery of the Scriptures, the Lord means that the pure in heart shall truly experience the presence of God both in this age and in the age to come.

In using this image of "seeing" God, Jesus was also drawing upon the rich imagery of the Old Testament. The great personalities of the Old Testament did not see God with their physical eyes. Indeed, we are reminded in the book of Exodus that no one can see God and live (Exodus 33:20). At the same time, however, we are told that the Lord "appeared" to Abraham (Genesis 12:7), that the Lord knew Moses "face to face" (Deuteronomy 34:10) and that Isaiah had a "vision of God" on his throne (Isaiah 6:1). These images point to the fact that these faithful leaders of Ancient Israel had an experience of the Living God which was deeply personal and affected their entire being.

The experience of the faithful people of ancient Israel was not one destined for them alone. It is the gift which was promised to all those faithful men and women who were wholly committed to God and who stood before him with integrity and true devotion. The Psalmist expresses the longing of all the faithful men and women when he writes: "My reward will be to see your face on rising, to enjoy the sight of your glory" (Psalm 17 [16]:15).

The profound experience of encounter with God, which is referred to as "seeing God" or experiencing God "face to face" is certainly one which can not be expressed adequately with human words. The words point to a deeper reality. Since it is an encounter of persons, the divine and the human, it is an event of love and an experience which cannot be defined. It is an experience expressed in our limited human language which respects the mysterious character of the event.

With this in mind, many of the great teachers of the Church have spoken of a number of distinct yet interrelated ways in with those who are faithful and "pure in heart" come to experience the presence of God.

First, those who are pure in heart experience the presence of God in other human persons. Created in the "image and likeness" (Genesis 1:26) of God, every person not only has an inherent dignity and identity but also has the potential to reveal the inherent the presence of God in their being. Christians believe, therefore, that the dignity and value of a person is not based upon age or abilities, not on social or economic status. It is not even based upon a persons religious convictions or morality. The dignity and value is God given. And, while the dignity may be covered through sin, it can never be eradicated. This is the truth expressed in the life and teachings of Jesus.

Those who are pure in heart know this truth and are able to "see" God in the other person regardless of his or her apparent position in life or in the outward quality of life. The human person, says Saint John Chrysostom, is "more precious in the eyes of God than any other creature. For him, the earth, the sea and the rest of creation exist."[3] Those who are pure in heart know that the Lord is revealed not only in the prominent but also "in the least" of the brethren (Matthew 25:40). There is no greater vision, says Saint Pachomius, than "to see the invisible God revealed in his temple, a visible human person."[4]

Second, those who are pure in heart also recognize that they are called to acknowledge their dignity and value as sons and daughters of God. They also have the potential to bear witness to the presence of God in their own lives and through the various circumstances of their life. Both the scriptures and the tradition of the Church use powerful terms to speak of the divine presence in our lives. The followers of Christ are meant to be "God's temple" (1 Corinthians 3:16) and members of the "body of Christ" (1 Corinthians 12:27). Speaking of those who struggle to follow Christ and live a virtuous life, Saint Gregory of Nyssa says: "So when people look at themselves they will see in themselves the One whom they are seeking. And this is the joy that will fill their purified heart."[5]

Third, those who are pure of heart experience the presence of God in and through the physical creation. The physical world is created by God. Although he is distinct from the creation, the Living God is intimately related to his creation. This means that the physical world can point to its creator and can reveal the presence of its creator to those who are pure in heart and have the eyes to see. Such persons know that "The heavens declare God's glory, and the work of his hands, the firmament proclaims" (Psalm 19 [18] :1).

And finally, those who are pure in heart experience the presence of God through worship and most especially through the Holy Eucharist. From the first days of Christianity, the followers of Christ have been a people who gather regularly for worship. The many dimensions of worship all point us towards a unique encounter with the Living God. The prayers and hymns, the reading of the Scriptures and the icons, the offering and receiving of the bread and wine are means through which the Triune God reveals himself to us through worship.

In describing the mysterious presence of God in others, in ourselves, in the creation and in worship, a number of Church fathers have spoken about a light which signifies the divine presence. The experience of this light is reminiscent of the event of our Lord's Transfiguration (Matthew 17:1-9). There on Mount Tabor, the three disciples experienced a the transfiguration of the Lord when his face was bright like the sun and his cloths became as white as light. A bright cloud of light enveloped Christ and overshadowed the mountain. It was as if the divinity of Christ seemed to penetrate his physical body in the form of light. The vivid light of the divine presence which the three disciples experienced has also been experienced by some followers of Christ through the ages.

Our experience of the presence of God in this life is real and genuine. We have the ability to truly know God in the present. Yet, these experiences of the Living God are never complete. Each experience has within it the genesis of a richer and deeper experience if we choose to grow ever closer to him. Each experience of God is like a flash of light which can only grow in intensity as we draw more closely to him. There is always greater illumination ahead of us.

The experiences of God in this life prepare us for those experiences of his presence which await those who are faithful on the other side of death. At that time, we shall be free from the stress and the strain, the contradictions and the pain, which frequently afflict our life in this world. Perhaps because of this, our ability to experience God in the life to come may even be greater. So, those who seek to know, to love, and to serve the Lord in this life look forward to the day when they will "see" the Lord even more clearly. With his help and guidance, we know that we called to progress ever more closely toward him in a movement of love which knows no boundary. With Saint Paul, we say with faith and hope that "no eye has seen, nor ear heard, nor heart of man conceived, what God has prepared for those who love him" (1 Corinthians 2:9).

Our Lord teaches us in the sixth Beatitude that those who come before God with a pure heart reflecting integrity and true devotion will have an experience of his presence. The experience of God is always one which enriches us and brings our life toward greater completion. This experience of God is one which is possible within the context of the relationships and responsibilities of this life for those who are pure in heart. It is an experience which will continue in the life to come. We shall be happy in the Lord.

From Our Christian Heritage

We can conceive then of no limitation in an infinite nature; and that which is limitless can not by its nature be understood. And so every desire for the Beautiful which draws us on in this ascent is intensified by the soul's very progress toward it. And this is the real meaning of seeing God; never to have the desire satisfied. But fixing our eyes on those things which help us see, we must ever keep alive in us the desire to see more and more. And so no limit can be set in our progress toward God; first of all because no limitation can be set on the Beautiful, and secondly because the increase in our desire for the Beautiful cannot be stopped by a sense of satisfaction.

Saint Gregory of Nyssa[6]

Prayer

Lord Jesus Christ! You told your disciples and apostles that many prophets and just ones had desired to see what they were seeing and to hear what they were hearing. So, now, count us worthy of hearing your words of salvation that, truly understanding them, we may bring fourth fruits worthy of their message. Enable us to adhere to truth and innocence of life and to persevere in goodness, lest we remain but passive recipients of this good news.

For you are the way, the truth, and the life, O Christ our God, and we give glory to you, your eternal Father, and your all-holy, good, and life-giving Spirit: now and forever, and unto ages of ages. Amen.

Chapter Seven

Blessed Are the Peacemakers For They Shall Be Called the Children of God

Jesus made his final journey to Jerusalem about three years after he began his public ministry. On that memorable day when he entered the capital city, there were many who welcomed the Lord. Some of these people recognized him to be the promised Messiah. Many of them must have heard him teaching about the Kingdom of God. Others were probably present when he cast out demons or healed those who were paralyzed. And so, as the Lord entered into the city seated upon a donkey, many of these people waved branches of the palm tree as an expression of their joy. Welcoming Jesus as the promised Messiah, they cried out: "Hosanna to the Son of David! Blessed is he who comes in the name of the Lord. Hosanna in the highest!" (Matthew 21:11).

Jesus was a person of peace. Through his words and actions, Jesus sought to bear witness to the love of God the Father for all. In obedience to the Father, Christ had come to restore us to the fellowship of God. His mission was one of reconciliation. Yet, his peaceful ways did not prevent the Lord from speaking the truth. He opposed sin in all its expressions and he challenged his listeners to turn away from their sinful ways. "The time is fulfilled and the kingdom of God is at hand;" he declared, "repent, and believe in the gospel" (Mark 1:15).

Because of his bold call to repentance, the Lord soon found

that there were those who not only opposed him but also were threatened by him. Not everyone received him as the Messiah and chose to accept his Gospel. Not everyone welcomed him with joy to the city of Jerusalem. Because of what the Lord said and because of what he did, there were those conspired to put him to death as a common criminal (Matthew 26:4). Many of these men were among the so-called religious leaders. Jesus had refused to overlook their arrogance and called them "blind guides" (Matthew 23:16). Indeed, he sharply rebuked them because of their hypocrisy (Matthew 23:23). Although the Lord called no one his enemy, there were those who made themselves his enemy and who chose not to receive him as the Messiah (John 1:11).

Not long after Jesus ate the "Last Supper" with his disciples, they all went to the garden of Gethsemane to pray. There, an angry crowd armed with swords and clubs surrounded Jesus and the disciples. Judas identified Jesus by kissing the Lord. The sign of love was turned into a sign of betrayal. As they began to take Jesus away, one of his disciples pulled out a sword and struck the slave of the high priest. Tensions were running high. This could have been the beginning of a bloody battle. But Jesus said: "No more of this! Put your sword back into its place; for all who take the sword will perish by the sword" (Luke 22:51, Matthew 26:53). Clearly, the Lord would have no part in violence.

The Peace of Christ

Our Lord Jesus Christ says to us in the seventh Beatitude: "Blessed are the peacemakers for they shall be called the children of God" (Matthew 5:9).

With these words, the Lord teaches that his disciples are makers of peace. As followers of Christ, we know that his coming was an event characterized by peace. In obedience to the Father, the Lord came in order to restore us to fellowship with God. He came to heal the divisions which are the result of sin. He came to unite us with the Father in a bond which cannot be broken by the forces of evil. He came "to guide our feet in the ways of peace" (Luke 1:79). Because of this, those of us who follow the Lord are meant to be the bearers of his peace, and active makers of peace

As it is used in the Scriptures, the word "peace" means much more that the mere absence of hostility and brokenness. It is a very rich and powerful word which signifies completeness and well-being. It refers to a condition of existence in which nothing essential is lacking.

The ancient Israelites believed that peace was a gift of God. It was the fruit of a life lived in fellowship with him. So, in ancient times, the normal greeting when two people met was the simple word "peace." It was both a greeting and a prayer that the other person would experience the peace of God.

Following his Resurrection, Jesus greeted his disciples with the words: "Peace be with you" (John 20:19). In the midst of their despair, the Apostles received the proclamation of peace from their Lord. It was a word both of assurance and well-being. His word was at once a declaration of the victory of God over the power of death and the invitation to abide by the gift of salvation.

This is the reason why the Apostle Paul could joyously proclaim: "We have peace with God through our Lord Jesus Christ" (Romans 5:1). Saint Paul knew that Christ had come to establish a new covenant between God and us. This is truly a covenant of peace because the Lord offers to all the healing, mercy, and forgiveness of God as well as the inspiration to love as he loves us.

Not all, however, are willing to receive Christ and the gift of peace which he brings. Even during his earthly life, there were those who freely chose not to receive Christ and the peace which he offered.

> This is the reason that Jesus once boldly de-
> clared: "Do you think that I have come to give
> peace on earth? No, I tell you but rather divi-
> sion; for henceforth in one house there will be
> five divided, three against two and two against
> three; they will be divided, father against son
> and son against father; mother against daugh-
> ter and daughter against mother..." (Luke
> 12:51-53).

There is clearly a paradox here. Jesus is truly the giver of peace. He says: "Peace I leave with you; my peace I give to you" (John 14:27). Yet, not all are ready and willing to accept him and, thereby, to receive his gift of peace.

The Gospel of Christ compels us to make a fundamental decision. We must decide whether we shall accept Christ as the Lord or whether we shall reject Christ. Because of this, there-fore, there may be division between those who have accepted Christ and those who have not. As the Lord says, this division may separate father from son and daughter from mother.

This sad division is not the desire of Christ. Rather, it is the consequence of our free will. We have the freedom either to accept Christ or to reject him. Because of this, Christ can be-come a "cause" of division between those who receive him and those who do not. His teaching can be the basis for contention between those who choose not to abide by his word and those who reject it.

The prophet Isaiah described the Messiah as the "Prince of Peace" (Isaiah 9:6). And, this is truly a very accurate description of Christ. As our Savior, the Lord has come in order to rescue us from the forces of evil. As the Good Shepherd, he has come to heal our alienation from the Father and from one another. As our Teacher, Christ has come to teach us the most fundamental truths about God and ourselves. As we have already said so many times, the Lord teaches us that we are meant to live our life in harmony with God and with others. We are most fully human when we live in fellowship with God.

When we read the New Testament, we find the story of a number of persons who accepted Christ as the Messiah and who received the peace which he offered. We read about Mary Magdalene. We read about Zacchaeus the tax collector. We read about the thief on the cross. We read about Paul who persecuted Christians prior to his conversion. These are but a few of the many persons described in the New Testament who decided to accept the Lord and change their lives.

Prior to their acceptance of Christ, each of these persons appears to have lived broken lives which had little peace. Their lives were broken by various forms of sin. After coming to accept Christ as their Lord, their lives were dramatically changed for the better. They were spiritually healed and they acquired the peace which is the fruit of salvation realized through a relationship with the Lord. Through the words and actions of Christ, they came to know God as their loving Father. By uniting themselves with Christ, they came to realize that they were indeed the beloved children of the Father. By making the words of Christ their own, they came to live a new life. These persons came to know the "peace of God which surpasses all understanding" (Philippians 4:7).

The stories of the disciples found in the New Testament as well as the stories of pious women and men throughout the ages, are powerful testimonies to the fact that Christ has been active in the lives of countless people in so many different places and at so many different times. The saints of every age and of every place bear witness to the fact that the Lord has revealed himself in and through their lives. In opening up their life to the Lord, not only did they come to know the "peace of God" but also they became bearers of that peace within the society in which they lived. Their lives manifested the light of Christ.

The Lord is not a remote figure of history. He is the Risen Lord who is alive and present in our midst. As he did in the past, so also in the present he offers to each of us the peace which comes from abiding in him and living in accordance with his teaching. Today, he is just as truly the one through whom we may have peace with God (Romans 5:1) and the one who can guide us in the ways of peace (Luke 1:79). The same "peace of God" which was known by the saints in the past is meant to be experienced by us in the present.

Acquiring the Peace of Christ

How do we acquire the "peace of God"?

There is a paradox here as well. In order to acquire this peace, we do not set out to seek it. Rather, we must seek Christ in all things. As we have already said, the "peace of God" is the fruit of our relationship with him. It is a consequence of living in fellowship with God. The more that we grow in our relationship with the Lord, the greater will be the "peace of God" in our life. This occurs naturally as we deepen the bond between Christ and ourselves.

Saint Nicholas Cabasilas expresses this relationship between Christ and each of us when he says:

> Christ gives to human persons life and growth,
> nourishment and light and breath. He opens
> their eyes and gives them light and the power

to see. He gives to human persons the bread of life, and this bread is nothing else than himself. He is life for those who are living and a sweet scent for those who breath. He clothes those who desire to be clothed. He strengthens the traveler and he is the way. He is at once both the inn along the road and the destination of the journey. When we struggle, he struggles at our side. When we argue, he is the arbiter. And when we win the victory, he is the prize.[1]

The "peace of God" is truly the fruit of our fellowship with the Lord. This fellowship is strengthened through prayer and the reading of Scripture, through fasting and acts of love toward others. It is strengthened through our worthy reception of Holy Communion. Each time we receive Holy Communion, we strengthen the bond between ourselves and Christ as well as all those who are in Christ.

Together with these spiritual disciplines, we also have an obligation truly to take stock of our life. Such an examination must have as its immediate goal the elimination of any form of sinful behavior and the establishment of a daily routine which is harmonious with our Christian convictions. We cannot hope to be blessed with the "peace of God" unless we recognize that "God has called us to peace" (1 Corinthians 7:15). We need consciously to strive to eliminate all forms of ill will, anger, hatred, and envy. We must be willing to forgive others as God has forgiven us. Saint Paul reminds us of our responsibility to be "imitators of God" when he says:

> Let all bitterness and wrath and anger and slander be put away from you with all malice, and be kind to another, tenderhearted, forgiving one another, as God in Christ forgave you. There-

> fore, be imitators of God as beloved children.
> And walk in love, as Christ loved us and gave
> himself up for us, a fragrant offering and sacri-
> fice to God. (Ephesians 4:31-5:2)

As we seek to eliminate all forms of sinful behavior, we must also look for opportunities to simplify our lives. Few of us would deny that our lives are not hectic and complicated. Although we have been richly blessed with many technological conveniences to make life easier, we find that our lives continue to become more complex. The relationships which we have with those we love frequently suffer due to lack of attention. Our responsibilities often increase to such a degree that we seem overwhelmed by them. For some of us, our lives appear to be out of our control.

When we live at a frenzied pace, it is difficult, if not impossible, to experience the "peace of God" in our life. Although we may be engaged in spiritual disciplines and striving to live a Christ-like life, the fact that our lives have a turbulent character to them often prevents us from experiencing the presence of the Lord and the peace which he brings.

So, many of us have a critical need not only to examine our lives but also to make changes in our schedules. Many of us need to reorder our daily routine in such a manner that our relationships are more meaningful and our responsibilities are more manageable. This reordering of our daily routine should allow time especially for prayerful meditation and retreats through which we can peacefully reflect upon our life and the activity of God in our lives. It should also allow us to have sufficient time to cultivate deeper relationships with those close to us.

We need to remember that the follower of Christ is not immune to difficulties. Nowhere in the Gospel does Christ teach that his followers will somehow be free from personal pain, temptations, hard choices, sorrow, or difficulties. Indeed, the Lord has told us that we would have troubles in our lives (John 16:33). Because we are human persons living in the world, involved in relationships and having responsibilities, we are always prone to encounter difficulties in our lives. In addition to this, we also know that discipleship may in fact bring upon the followers of the Lord added difficulties because of their relationship with Christ. The disciples may be prone to ridicule, persecution, and slander because of their devotion to Christ and their decision to abide by his Gospel (Matthew 5:11).

Having been gifted with the "peace of God," the followers of Christ are in a distinctive position to face the difficulties which may come their way. We know that these difficulties do not come from God. God certainly does not inflict evils upon anyone. We also know that, because of our relationship with God, we are assured of his fatherly care. As his sons and daughters, we receive from him the resources necessary to face these difficulties. It is for this very reason that the Lord says:

> "Therefore, I tell you do not be anxious about your life, what you shall eat or what you shall drink, not about your body, what you shall put on. Is not life more than food, and the body more than clothing. Look at the birds of the air: they neither sow nor reap nor gather into barns, and yet your heavenly father feeds them. Are you not of more value than they?" (Matthew 6:25-26).

These are simple words. But they express a profound truth. Jesus is telling us that we are valued by God our Father. He knows our needs and our concerns. Although we may sometimes neglect him, God never neglects us. He is well aware of our concerns and the difficulties which we face in life. And, as our loving Father, he is always ready to provide us with what we truly need.

Jesus recognized that we would be prone to difficulties. Our Lord knew that reality often confronts us with troubles which are not our own making. Yet, he drew a very important distinction between the external difficulties which we may encounter and our inner life. Although we may face very real external problems and difficulties, our inner disposition can remain peaceful in so far as we are living in fellowship with him. Our hearts need not be troubled if we truly believe in him, abide in his love, and follow his teachings (John 14:1).

We should remember also that the Lord tells us that the peace which he gives to us is "not of this world." With this simple qualification, Christ is telling us that the peace which he offers as the fruit of reconciliation is different from what we may imagine it to be. The peace which the Lord offers to us is not simply the momentary feeling of contentment. Such a feeling is emotional in nature and is generally conditioned by the immediate circumstances in which we find ourselves. The peace which the Lord offers us is an inner experience and realization that we belong to God and that we are living in fellowship with him. This new reality of peace is not the result of external circumstances which affect our emotions. Rather, it is the fruit of our relationship with God which is rooted in the reality of Christ's activity in our life and nurtured by the Spirit.

This is the "peace of God" which can characterize our lives even when we find ourselves surrounded by turmoil and confronted with difficulties. It is an inner state of well-being which is present even in the face of disappointment, sickness, sorrow or troubles.

A particular quality of persons who abide in this kind of peace is a strong yet subtle wholeness of character. While maintaining their personal uniqueness, these persons are not easily swayed with the fickle fads and priorities which sometimes mark the society around us. Under no circumstances do these persons of peace make others of good will feel religiously inferior or spiritually shamed. Rather than projecting to others contrived impressions of "religiosity," "spirituality" or "peace," these persons instead are so "easy to be around." These persons bear within themselves a kind of wholesomeness which is essential to their being.

The Makers of Peace

The disciples of Christ are offered the "peace of God" as a gift resulting from our relationship with the Lord. At the same time, the disciples of Christ are also called to be the makers of peace in the world. This is very clear from the words of the Lord. He does not say: "Blessed are the peaceful." Rather, he says: "Blessed are the peacemakers." Certainly, the Lord wants his followers to live their lives in a peaceful manner. He wants us to experience the inner realization of peace which is rooted in the salvation which he brings. Yet, if we look carefully at the Beatitude, the Lord proclaims a blessing upon those who are "makers of peace." He wants his followers not only to abide in his peace but also to be the instruments of his peace.

Some historians and students of past civilizations might very well tell us that we do not live in a very violent society compared to those of other places and ages. This may be a comforting observation. Without minimizing the tragic acts of violence which do occur, it may indicate that the Gospel of Christ has had some measure of influence upon our society and upon a number of others in today's world.

Yet, this observation should not prevent us from recognizing the harsh fact that various forms of violence do exist within our society. Most of us recognize that violence is not an acceptable means toward an end. Yet there are some who freely choose to act in a violent manner in order to gain a particular end. Their violent behavior not only hurts others but also ultimately hurts themselves. Violence is a tragic aspect of our society.

Violence can take a number of forms. It can be very obvious or very subtle. The physical abuse of another person is a tragic expression of violence. But, it is but one expression of violence. Persons can also be abused in an emotional manner or in a spiritual manner. Persons can be wounded with guns and knives. Persons can also be wounded with harassment and words of hate. Persons can be hurt by lack of love and by neglect.

Violence is not restricted to darkened alleys. We also know that violent situations can flare up in our homes, at our workplace, at school, at sporting events, on the highway, and even at play. Some of these situations may involve strangers who were simply brought together by circumstances. Other violent situations may involve members of the same family, neighbors, colleagues at work, or leaders from within our own community.

We also need to recognize how easily we can become accosted by the vision of violence. In order to gain a larger audience and greater profits, some television shows and movies seem to propagate violence. In order to attract our attention, commercials and advertisements can easily diminish the dignity of the human person with violent images. Violence is sometimes portrayed as a acceptable means to an end.

Christians are obliged to recognize that all forms of violence are contrary to the teachings of our Lord. While the followers of Christ may be prone to search for the psychological and sociological factors which contribute to violent behavior, we are bound to acknowledge that the Gospel of Christ does not provide any justification for violence. Indeed, if Jesus chose to act in an non-violent manner, then his followers have an obligation to follow his example.

This means that the followers of Christ have the obligation to renounce all forms of violence and faithfully to commit ourselves to be the makers of peace. If we claim to follow the "Prince of Peace," then we certainly must be committed to the process of healing brokenness. The activity of the "Prince of Peace" must be ours as well.

There is a very real relationship between the realization of the peace of Christ in our life and our obligation to share this peace with others. As with every gift which we receive from God, it is a gift which is meant not only to enrich our life but also to enrich the lives of others. If we have become the recipients of the "peace of God," we are also its stewards. The peace with which we have been blessed must be shared with others. Reminding us of this fact, Saint Gregory of Nyssa speaks about the significance of Christ's gift of peace when he says:

> Peace is indeed the greatest of the things which give joy; and this he wishes each of us to have in such measure as to keep it not only for one's self but also to be able to dispense from the overflow of one's abundance to others. For he says: 'Blessed are the peacemakers.' Now a peacemaker is a person who gives peace to another. But, one cannot give to another what one does not possess. So, the Lord wants first that you be filled with the blessing of peace, and then communicate it to those who have need of it.[2]

Choosing to be a "maker of peace" is a daring and courageous act. It is an act which reflects our devotion to Christ and his Gospel. It is an act which also recognizes that violence only yields violence. In choosing to be a "maker of peace," the followers of Christ affirm that they are committed to be persons of reconciliation, to be the bearers of goodness, and to be the witnesses to the presence of the Lord. The followers of Christ recognize that tensions and conflicts can not be resolved by violence but with justice, compassion, and love. We must, as Saint Paul says, "follow after those things which make for peace" (Romans 14:19).

The requirements of the peacemaker have been beautifully expressed in the following prayer composed by Saint Francis of Assisi.

> Lord, make me an instrument of your peace.
> Where there is sorrow, let me sow love.
> Where there is injury, pardon.
> Where there is doubt, faith.
> Where there is despair, hope.
> Where there is darkness, light.
> Where there is sadness, joy.
>
> O Divine Master,
> Grant that I may not so much seek
>   to be consoled
> as to console.
> To be understood, as to understand.
> To be loved, as to love.
> For it is giving that we receive.
> It is in pardoning that we are pardoned.
> And it is in dying that we are born
>   to eternal life.

Recited by Christians for over seven hundred years, this powerful prayer of Saint Francis reminds us of another important characteristic of the peacemaker. While we have an obligation to be instruments of peace, we also have an obligation to eradicate those evils which can provide a basis for violent behavior. While we are bound to recognize that all forms of violence are evil, we are also obliged to recognize that violence is frequently fostered by other evils which can easily alter in a negative way a person's values and perception of life.

The lack of love, the absence of hope, the denial of justice can frequently provide the basis for violent behavior. Persons who lack the basic necessities for life or who have been treated unjustly, or who have been discriminated against can easily be tempted to turn to violence in a desperate attempt to redress their grievance.

Guided by the Holy Spirit, the makers of peace have an obligation, therefore, not only to recognize these deficiencies but also to work for the elimination of those societal evils which can do damage to the lives of persons. Viewed from the perspective of the Gospel, our lives are intimately related. Those who suffer from violence, war, discrimination, injustice, starvation, and deprivation are not strangers. They are our brothers and sisters. They share with us a common God and Father. If we have come to sense even in a small measure the "peace of God" then we have an obligation to our brothers and sisters to do all we can so that they too will have the opportunity to know and love the "Prince of Peace."

After speaking of the tragic consequences upon human affairs of such evils as wrath, envy and hypocrisy; Saint Gregory of Nyssa says:

> So, a person who eliminates such a sickness from human life and unites the members of humanity by peace and goodwill truly performs a work of divine power. Such a person banishes the evils of the human condition and introduces instead

a portion of what is good. For this reason Christ calls the peacemaker a child of God because the person imitates the true God who endows human life with these blessings.

Therefore, blessed are the peacemakers for they shall be called the children of God! Who are these persons? They are those who imitate the love of God for humankind, who reveal in their own live the characteristics of God's activity. The Lord and Giver of good things completely annihilates anything that is without affinity and foreign to goodness. This work he also directs for you. Namely, to cast out hatred and abolish war, to exterminate envy and banish strife, to get rid of hypocrisy, and to extinguish from within resentment of injuries which linger in the heart.[3]

Saint Gregory reminds us with these powerful words that our Lord did not intend for his followers to be oblivious to the real difficulties of the society in which we live. Rather, the Lord directs us to be the "salt of the earth" and the "light of the world" (Matthew 5:13-14). As the Lord came into this world for the sake of its salvation, so we who bear his name also live in the world as persons working for its salvation. With values rooted in the Gospel of Christ, we are meant to be persons who reflect the presence of the Lord in this world. We are challenged to preserve that which is good, to oppose what is evil, and to illumine the way for those who seek the good.

So, with this Beatitude in mind, the followers of the Lord certainly are called to recognize our obligation to be both bearers of the peace of God and makers of peace in our homes, at our workplace, in our neighborhood, and in our country. Indeed, as citizens, the followers of the Lord have a special responsibility to encourage a national policy which not only emphasizes the need for world peace but also seeks to eliminate those factors which provide the basis for divisions among peoples and for international hostility.

The Blessing of Being Called the Children of God

Our Lord Jesus Christ declares in the seventh Beatitude that the peacemakers will be called the children of God.

There are many titles which are used in the Scriptures and Tradition of the Church to describe those persons who are living their life in accordance with the Gospel of Christ.

Among the many titles, the followers of the Lord are frequently referred to as the "servants of God," (Romans 6:22), as the "heirs of God" (Romans 6:17), and as the "friends of Christ" (John 15:15). Certainly, all of these titles are valuable because they help us to better understand a particular aspect of our relationship with God and his relationship with each of us.

Yet, there is a special honor to being called the children of God. These words are meant to remind us that there is a deeply personal relationship between God and each of us.

In order to emphasize this personal relationship we have with God, Jesus taught not only that we are the children, the sons and daughters, of God but also that God is "our Father" (Matthew 6:9). He has taught us that the Father knows each of us and loves each of us in a deeply personal way. An old Christian axiom attributed to Saint Augustine says: "God loves each one of us as if there were only one of us." His love is deeply personal. It is a love which is always free and unconditional. It is always a love offered to us in order to enhance our unique identity as persons created in his "image and likeness" (Genesis 1:26). The Father never treats us as strangers. Rather, he always honors us as his sons and daughters.

The children of God will be known as peacemakers. Jesus declares this because it is through the making of peace that the sons and daughters of God will manifest their true identity. Because of God's mysterious love, we belong to him as his sons and daughters. Yet, we are called daily to be led by the Spirit and manifest this dignity (Romans 8:14). We are called daily to live our lives as his sons and daughters in a manner which brings glory to him.

This means that we can not claim to be the sons and daughters of God unless we actively promote the process of peace. We are called to be the instruments of God's peace by truly being the bearers of his healing and reconciliation. We know that "God was in Christ reconciling the world to himself and he has given to us the ministry of reconciliation" (2 Corinthians 5:18-19). Those of us who truly live our lives as makers of peace will indeed experience the blessing of being the sons and daughters of God. We will know what it means to be not simply the servants but the sons and daughters of the Most High God (Acts 16:17).

Our Lord teaches us in the seventh Beatitude that those who are the makers of peace are the ones who have experienced the gift of the peace of God. Because of this, we are meant to be persons of reconciliation, honored with the dignity of being the sons and daughters of God. We shall be happy in the Lord.

From Our Christian Heritage

Do all you can to love everyone. If you are not yet able to, at the very least do not hate anyone. Yet you will not even manage this if you have not reached detachment from the things of this world.

You must love everyone with all your soul, hoping, however, only in God and honoring him with all your heart.

Christ's friends are not loved by all, but they sincerely love all. The friends of this world are not loved by all, but neither do they love all. Christ's friends persevere in their love right to the end. The friends of this world persevere only so long as they do not find themselves in disagreement over worldly matters.

A faithful friend is an effective protector. When things are going well, he gives you good advice and shows you his sympathy in practical ways. When things are going badly, he defends you unselfishly and he is a deeply committed ally.

Many people have said many things about love. But if you are looking for it, you will only find it in the followers of Christ. Only they have true Love as their teacher in love.

This is the Love about which it is written: 'If I have prophetic powers, and understand all mysteries and all knowledge, but have not love, I am nothing" (1 Corinthians 13:2).

Whoever has love has God, because God is Love (1 John 4:16).

St. Maximos the Confessor[4]

Prayer

O Lord, who bless those who bless you and sanctify those who trust in you: Save your people and bless your inheritance! Preserve the fullness of your Church and sanctify those who love the beauty of your house. Honor them, in return, with your divine might and do not desert us who trust in you. Give peace to this world of yours, to your Churches, to the clergy, to our country, and to all your people. For the giving of every gift is accomplished perfectly in heaven above and descends from you, the Father of lights, and we give you glory, thanksgiving and adoration, Father, Son, and Holy Spirit: now and forever, and unto ages of ages.

Chapter Eight

Blessed Are Those Who Are Persecuted For Righteousness' Sake For Theirs Is the Kingdom of Heaven

Jesus sought to harm no one. He was a person of righteousness. Obedient to his Father, the Lord came into our midst in order to restore us to fellowship with God. Jesus spoke of the infinite love which God has for us. He also taught us that our love for God and for one another are the most important virtues of our life. In his dealings with others, he always acted in a virtuous manner.

Yet, his words we not heard by all. His actions were not honored by all. While there were many who did in fact receive him as the promised Messiah and chose to follow him, there were others who refused to accept the Lord. They were threatened by the righteousness of Christ and the truthfulness of his words. In all things, the Lord sought to do what was right. He always spoke the truth. Almost from the very beginning of his ministry, therefore, there were those who sought to be rid of Jesus.

After about three years of his public ministry, the Lord was betrayed by one of his own disciples. He was arrested and brought before the Sanhedrin which was the assembly of religious leaders in Palestine. The Lord was accused of blasphemy by those who claimed to hear his teaching. Many bore false witness against him. Yes, those who professed to be the teachers of religion condemned the Lord to death (Matthew 26:65-68).

In preparation for his crucifixion, the Lord was flogged and mocked. He was spit upon, stripped, and dressed in a scarlet tunic. A crown of thorns was placed on his head as the soldiers sarcastically called him the "King of the Jews" (Matthew 27:29). Having experienced all of this, Christ was then given a large cross bar which he had to carry through the streets of Jerusalem leading to the hill of Calvary where he was to be put to death

Crucifixion was the most brutal form of capital punishment in the ancient world. This is so because the person who was crucified would usually hang on the cross in agony for hours before death finally came from suffocation. This is exactly what happened in the case of Christ. For about three hours, he hung upon the cross. During this period of time, he was ridiculed over and over again by many of those who came to witness the event. Most of his friends had abandoned him in fear. Only Mary his mother and John, the youngest Apostle, remained at the foot of the cross.

Throughout this ordeal, however, the Lord spoke no words of anger or retribution. His trust was in God the Father. As the moment of death had arrived, Jesus prayed for those who persecuted him. He said: "Father forgive them for they know not what they do" (Luke 23:34).

The Call to Discipleship

Our Lord says to us in the eighth Beatitude: "Blessed are those persecuted for righteousness' sake, for theirs is the Kingdom of Heaven" (Matthew 5:10).

With these words, the Lord teaches that his disciples are persons who will be abused because of their convictions and their actions. Virtue will not always be honored and recognized.

As the Lord was abused by those who rejected him and his teachings, the follower of Christ will be also prone to ridicule, persecution, and slander.

Jesus Christ has called each of us to be his disciple. As he called to the first Apostles along the side of the Sea of Galilee nearly two thousand years ego, so also the Risen Lord continues to call persons of every age, in every place, and of every stage of personal development to follow him. As he said to the first Apostles, so also he says to each of us: "Come, and follow me" (Matthew 19:21).

Each of us has our own weaknesses and inadequacies. None of us can honestly say that we are prepared to be a disciple. Yet, the Lord meets us where we are. He affirms that we are the daughters and sons of the Father. He invites each of us follow him, to share in his life, and to be heralds of his Gospel.

Bound through faith and love with all those who are united with Christ, each of us is called by the Lord to a life of discipleship characterized by the love of God and the love of neighbor (Matthew 22:36-40). Through our union with Christ, we are able to realize our distinct and personal identity as a daughter or son of God and to live a life which gives glory to our Father in heaven (Matthew 5:16).

Our life of discipleship begins in a solemn and public manner with Baptism. At the time of our baptism, the Lord claims us in a special way. Through the waters of baptism, we are set apart publicly to be his disciples and to be bearers of the Gospel. From this time onward, the Lord calls us to realize our fundamental identity as a daughter or son of God through fellowship with him. As at the first Pentecost, the Holy Spirit comes to dwell in us and to empower us to live the life of discipleship by conforming us to the image of Christ (Romans 8:29). The actions of God makes each of us one of the followers of Christ not in virtue of our merit but in virtue of his love. God, as Saint Paul says, "has saved us and called us to be holy not because of anything we ourselves have done but for his own purpose and by his own grace" (2 Timothy 1:9).

Saint Cyprian of Carthage speaks of the bond between the believer and Christ established at baptism when he says:

> All our power for good is God's gift; he is the source of our life and strength. Through him we grow and mature so as to experience in this life a foretaste of what is to come. Only let us keep our hearts pure, and fear nothing so much as to loose our newly restored innocence; then the Lord who has made the light of his grace shine in our hearts will establish his home within us. If we walk firmly and steadily in the Lord's ways, trusting in him with all our heart and strength, all we have to do is be what our baptism has made us. Freedom and power to do good will be given us in proportion to our spiritual growth. God does not measure his heavenly gifts to us in the scales the way we mortals dispense earthly goods; he pours out his Spirit without stint, so that it flows freely on and on, never ceasing, continually abounding in endless generosity.[1]

As followers of the Lord, we have been entrusted with both a message and a mission. Our message is the love of God. We are meant to proclaim in both our words and deeds that "God so loved the world that he sent his only son, that whoever believes in him should not perish but have eternal life" (John 3:16). This message is the Gospel of salvation which the Lord has entrusted to his disciples. It is a message which is not to be kept to ourselves. Rather, it is a message which is meant to be proclaimed throughout the world (Matthew 16:15).

We also have a mission. As followers of the Lord, we share in his mission of reconciliation. The Lord has come in order to restore us to fellowship with the Father. Despite the fact that we can so easily alienate ourselves from God through our lack of faithful love, Christ has come to reconcile us with the Father. As persons who count ourselves reconciled to the Father through Christ, we have been entrusted with the ministry of reconciliation. Our task is to bear witness to the healing love and mercy of God. Following the example of our Lord, we are called to be persons of reconciliation.

Each of us must freely accept the action of God in our life. The Lord has called us to be his disciples. He has invited us to be his friends and co-workers. Yet, he does not force us to love him or to accept his invitation. The Lord respects the fact that we are human persons gifted with free will. Although we may in fact be baptized, we always have the freedom at every point in our life either to respond to the Lord or to reject his invitation. Even during his earthly ministry, there were those who encountered Christ but who choose not to accept the words of Christ and not to follow him.

The life of the disciple is meant to be characterized by joy. This sense of joy is an expression of the fact that we are bound to Christ and that we see ourselves as his follower and friend (John 15:11). It is the joy of knowing that we have found the "pearl of great price" (Matthew 11:46), which is the treasure of the Kingdom of Heaven (Matthew 13:44). It is the joy of knowing that we receive the words of Christ (John 3:29) and share in his ministry of reconciliation (Luke 10:17). Because it is rooted in our relationship with the Lord, this is the joy which is present even in the face of challenge and great difficulty (James 1:2).

The Cost of Discipleship

Being a follower of Christ is not always easy. While the life of the disciple is meant to be characterized by a sense of joy, this does not mean that it will be a life free from difficulties. The Lord never told us that our lives would be free from difficulties. He never said that his disciples would not be subject to challenges which could sorely test their fortitude and commitment. On the contrary, the Lord clearly says that his followers would be persecuted because of their message and their mission. He says to all those who seek to follow him: "If they persecute me, they will persecute you" (John 15:20).

According to the teachings of our Lord, the disciple is prone to at least three forms of abuse. These are ridicule, persecution, and slander (Matthew 4:11). Each type of abuse is intended to separate the disciple from the Lord. Each type of abuse can cause great pain, both physical and psychological, for the disciple who is its victim.

Ridicule is a form of abuse in which words are used to express contempt or disparagement. We know that our Lord was ridiculed by the soldiers as they prepared him for the journey to Calvary. They mocked the Lord saying: "Hail King of the Jews" as they struck him an spat upon him. (Matthew 27:29-30). Later, as our Lord hung upon the cross, people in the crowd cried our with contempt saying: "You who would destroy the Temple and build it in three days, save yourself" (Matthew 27:40). There were others who cried out: "He saved others; he cannot save himself. He is the King of Israel let him come down from the cross and we will believe in him. He trusts in God; let God deliver him now, if he desires him; for he said I am the Son of God" (Matthew 27:42). Our Lord certainly heard these evil words; but, he chose not to respond.

Few of us have not experienced the pain of ridicule. We know the genuine agony which is produced in us when we become the object of sarcasm or contempt.

As the followers of the Lord, we are susceptible to ridicule simply because of our faith commitment. Those who ridicule Christians often do so by speaking with contempt about our convictions, by scorning our values, and by disparaging our religious practices. Frequently, there is an attempt to make the followers of the Lord feel ignorant or backwards because of our belief in God and our commitment to the Christian way of life.

Persecution is the second form of abuse which the Lord said would be inflicted upon his followers. Persecution is a broad term which can include a number of various forms of physical or psychological injury inflicted upon a person. We know that Jesus was persecuted in many ways.

When we read about the events leading up to his crucifixion, we find examples of many types of physical and psychological persecution directed against him. The Lord was falsely accused and humiliated. He was mocked by his detractors and abandoned by most of his friends. He was spit upon, stripped naked, beaten, and tortured. He was crucified as a common criminal between two thieves. Bearing all of this "as a lamb led to the slaughter," the Lord chose not to return evil to his persecutors (Isaiah 53:7).

Few of us have not experienced some form of persecution. Some of us know the agony of physical pain inflicted upon us by those whose hearts were filled with anger, fear or envy. Most of us know the emotional pain which results from false accusations, rejection, discrimination or acts of injustice.

As the followers of Christ, we are also susceptible to persecution simply because of our faith commitment. In some parts of the world today, Christians suffer from physical persecution because of their faith. There are places where Christian believers are prone to physical torture because of their desire to follow Christ and their unwillingness to condone evil. Elsewhere, Christians are often prone to various forms of psychological persecution because of the same convictions. This form of persecution is directed against the spirit of a person. Because of our faith convictions, some of us are victims of forms of psychological persecution such as rejection and discrimination. While this type of persecution does not always produce some form of external injury, the pain which is experienced by the believer is very real.

Slander is the third form of abuse which the Lord said would be inflicted upon his followers. Slander is a false or distorted report about a person done with malice. Slander is meant to discredit a person by harming one's reputation. Our Lord was slandered by those who sought to discredit him and put him to death. Because he healed on the Sabbath, the Lord was accused of being a sinner (John 9:16). Because he showed his concern for the needy and less fortunate, the Lord was accused of being a glutton and a drunkard (Luke 19:7). After the Lord was arrested, the chief priests and elders found those who would make false accusations against Jesus. These false accusations were used as the basis for the judgment against him (Mark 14:57). Bearing these false accusations, Jesus, however, did not return evil for evil.

Few of us have not been the victim of slander in one form or another. Slander is a particularly evil form of verbal abuse because it attempts to damage or destroy a reputation through the malicious distortion or misinterpretation of what was said or what was done. It is, therefore, a form of abuse which can be easily be accomplished. The slanderer need only take out of context the statement or the action of another person. The good name and reputation of a good person can be easily tarnished in the eyes of others by the malicious action of a slanderer.

As followers of Christ, we can be the victims of slander because of our faith convictions. Our Christian beliefs and practices are not respected by all. Because we choose to follow the teachings of Christ, we may be accused of being backwards. Because we recognize the value of prayer, we can easily be accused of being naive. Because we choose to be peacemakers, we can easily be accused of being cowards. We are called to let our faith be the basis for all our actions. Whenever we take a position on a subject which reflects our faith and which is contrary to the opinions of others, we may indeed become the victims of the vicious distortions of a slanderer. It is for this reason that Saint Paul says that "all who desire to live a godly life in Christ Jesus will be persecuted" (2 Timothy 3:12).

The Sign of the Cross

The reality of the cross always stands before every follower of Christ. When we look at the cross, we are reminded of the profound love which God has for us. The cross stands as a sign of that love, as a token of God's victorious love which is more powerful than sin and death. Yet, we cannot look at the cross without also being reminded of all the suffering which our Lord endured for the sake of our salvation. Long before the Lord picked up the wooden cross to carry up the hill of Calvary, he had come to bear a number of other crosses. He knew the pain of a cross when he was rejected by so many whom he came to save. He knew the pain of a cross when he was falsely accused. He knew the pain of a cross when he was betrayed by one of his own disciples.

For this reason, the Lord has associated the cross with discipleship. He says: "If anyone would come after me let him deny

himself and take up his cross and follow me" (Matthew 16:24).
With these simple yet forceful words the Lord tells us that discipleship involves ridding ourselves of selfishness. The disciple
is one whose life is centered upon God and not on self. Indeed,
it is only through living in fellowship with God that we come
to recognize our true self. This is why the Lord says: "For whoever would save his life will loose it, and whoever loses his life
for my sake will find it" (Matthew 16:26).

The Lord also tells us that the disciple is also one who bears
a cross. Being a follower of Christ means that we can very well
be the victims of abuse and bear the cross of ridicule, persecution, and slander. While we seek to live peacefully with all
persons, the Christian must recognize the hard fact that our faith
convictions are not shared by all.

Each time we say the "Our Father," or recite the Nicene
Creed, we are reminded that we profess specific convictions
about God, ourselves, others, and the world in which we live.
These faith convictions provide Christians with a distinctive
perspective on life. Often, our faith convictions demand that
we behave in a manner which is different from others in our
society. Our beliefs are expressed in the way we behave. We are
called to live daily a life worthy of our vocation of being sons
and daughters of God. Because of this, we may find ourselves
to be the victims of ridicule, persecution, and slander. In bearing these evils, we come to "have some share on the sufferings
of Christ" (1 Peter 4:13).

Our Lord was a victim of abuse from the very persons he
had come to save. He knew ridicule, persecution, and slander.
Yet, the Lord never responded in like manner to these evils. In
each of his encounters with evil, Christ freely choose to manifest the power of God. Christ responded to evil with love, with
mercy, with forgiveness. The Lord refused to let the evil deed

of another become the justification for further evil. The Lord knew that there could be no justification for evil. Because of this, Christ bore the evil which was sent his way and, thereby, destroyed its power.

Saint Innocent of Alaska reminds us of the suffering of Christ and the manner in which he bore the abuse when he says:

> With unspeakable meekness and love did Jesus Christ endure every insult. He never complained to those who offended him, or grew angry at even the worst of his enemies, those who slandered, mocked, and sought to kill him. A single word from his mouth would have sufficed to kill and annihilate all his enemies and opponents, Yet, such was not his desire. On the contrary, he wished them well, did good to them, prayed for them, and wept when he saw that they were nonetheless perishing. In brief, from birth to death, Jesus Christ never sinned at all in word, deed, or thought, but in all things and at all times did good to all people.[2]

The example of the Lord clearly shows us that we have no right to abuse those who abuse us. As the followers of the Lord, we have no right to ridicule, persecute or slander those who are engaged in such tactics.

The Lord tells us how we are meant to respond to those who abuse us when he says:

> You have heard it was said, 'You shall love your neighbor but hate your enemy.' But I say to you, Love your enemies and pray for those who persecute you...
>
> But I say to you that hear, Love your enemies, do good to those who hate you, bless those who

> curse you, pray for those who abuse you. To him
> who strikes you on the cheek, offer the other
> also; and from him who takes away your cloak
> do not withhold your coat as well... Love your
> enemies, and do good, expecting nothing in re-
> turn, and your reward will be great, and you
> will be sons of the Most High; for he is kind to
> the ungrateful and selfish. Be merciful, even as
> your Father is merciful. (Matthew 5:43-44, Luke
> 6:27-37)

Despite the gravity of the abuses which are directed against us, we are not meant to return evil for evil. When we behave in an evil manner or speak in an evil way, we only contribute to the power of evil. It is as if we become an accomplice to the forces which struggle against God. When we respond to evil with good, on the other hand, we break the power of evil. We do not give it any further authority. And, we remain faithful to our vocation to live our life as the sons and daughters of God.

Because of our convictions about God and his saving actions, we have a distinctive understanding of ourselves and the world in which we live. As we have repeatedly said in our discussion of the Beatitudes, we also have a particular way of living our life as the followers of the Lord. Although we may be the victims of ridicule, persecution and slander, we have no right to be the instigators of these. We must avoid returning evil for evil. We must avoid becoming persecutors of those who have harmed us.

This applies to each of us as persons. And, it also applies to us as a community of Christians. Sadly, there have been times when Christians have joined with the forces of governments in order to persecute those persons who held different religious or political views. Despite the many sad examples from history, contemporary Christians must recognize that we have no right to become "persecutors" in the name of Christ. Even though we have come to experience persecution because of our convictions, we have no right use violence in order to proclaim the Gospel.

Yes, the Lord has taught us to preach the Gospel to every people throughout the world. However, he has not directed us to impose the Christian faith on others by force or by the threat of violence. While we are obliged to bear witness to our faith, we are also obliged to respect the dignity of other persons and to honor their convictions.

Saint Basil the Great reflects the teaching of the Lord when he says:

> Do not cure evil by evil, nor strive to outdo one another in inflicting injuries. For in such evil strife, he who wins is more to be pitied, for he goes away bearing the greater part of the blame. Do not pile up the debt of your own wickedness; do not make an evil debt more evil. Does someone in rage insult you? Bear with the offense in silence. Instead, you gather into your heart the evil food of his wrath; you imitate the winds that throw back whatever is throne against them. Do not let your enemy become your teacher; and do not strive to become what you detest. Beware, lest you become the mirror of an angry person, reflecting his image in yourself. [3]

The final words of Saint Basil remind us also of the danger of letting anger get the best of us. We all have experienced anger. When we are hurt by another person, we feel anger. When we are insulted, we feel anger. When we are misled by someone, we feel anger. When we are confronted with any form of abuse from others, we react with the feeling of anger.

When we become angry, our entire being seems involved in the reaction. While we might at first say that anger is an emotional reaction to something which we do not like, we must recognize that it is also a physical reaction. Our heart may beat quicker. Blood may rush to our head. Our muscles may become tense. It seems that when we become angry our whole body is involved in a natural reaction to the hurt.

Some may argue that a Christian is not supposed to become angry. Such a view seems to be based upon the belief that all forms of anger are necessarily evil. This is not the case! It is not the anger which is evil in and of itself. Rather, there are particular ways which anger may be expressed or repressed which are sinful. There are ways of expressing anger which can truly do damage to us and to others, and alienate us from God. These are the expressions of anger are truly sinful. These particular expressions of anger may be called rage. When we are enraged, we immediately disconnect our conscious connection with our fundamental identity as sons and daughters of God. It is of paramount importance, then, to first " re-connect " with our genuine identity before we proceed with any other further decision or action which is associated with our anger.

The Gospels tell us that Jesus became angry on a number of occasions. When the Lord was challenged by those whose hearts were hardened, he was angry (Mark 3:1-5). When the Lord saw the money changers in the Temple, he expressed his anger (John 2:13-15). When he challenged the hypocrisy of the scribes and Pharisees, the Lord expressed his anger (Matthew 23). In each of these cases, the Lord's anger was a natural response to actions which were sinful. The Lord, however, did not permit his anger to be a cause of sin. He shows us that it is possible to be angry without falling into sin.

In his letter to the Ephesians, Saint Paul offers us some important and practical advice on anger. He says: "Be angry, but do not sin; do not let the sun go down on your anger, and give no opportunity to the devil" (Ephesians 4:26).

These words of Saint Paul provide us with the basis for dealing with anger properly. First, we are not meant permanently to repress anger. When we indefinitely repress anger, we may think that we are appearing calm and collected in the face of difficulty. Yet, this type of repression of anger may in fact lead us to sin. It often leads to progressively more evil thoughts directed toward another. It may serve as the basis for a growing inner rage which seems to "eat away" within us. Repressed anger can also "express" itself even through the cold way in which we may treat another person or in callous remarks or malicious jokes which defame another. Repressed anger can so easily lead to sin.

Second, we must seek to express our anger in an appropriate manner. Sin and evil should anger us. Injustice should anger us. Violence should anger us. Hypocrisy should anger us. However, this anger should not become the basis for resentment, arrogance, or self-righteousness. Anger should not become the justification for physical or emotional abuse of another. On the contrary, we need to be able to channel our anger in a manner which is constructive. We need to be willing to contribute to the elimination of sin and evil if it is within our power. Our anger can become the basis for a greater commitment to do good, a willingness to offer constructive directions to others as well as the patience to seek creative solutions to these and other difficulties. At the same time we need to recognize the necessity to pray for God's guidance.

And finally, we must be willing to act quickly. When anger is not expressed in an appropriate manner, it can easily become the basis for sin. We need to do our best to deal with problems in our relationships as quickly as we can, if it is realistically in our power to do so. Little arguments and disagreements can often lead to greater difficulties, if they are not attended to. Anger can easily turn to rage and resentment. This is the reason why Saint Paul says: "Do not let the sun go down on your anger and give no opportunity to the devil" (Ephesians 4:26).

The Lord does not abandon us in times of difficulty. He knows very well the abuse to which his disciples are prone. As our Lord and brother, Christ is near to those who are persecuted because of the sake of what is right.

Through the activity of the Holy Spirit, the Lord provides us with both the comfort, the fortitude and the wisdom to respond to the abuse directed against us. The gift of fortitude enables us not to respond to evil with evil. The gift of wisdom enables us to assess insightfully the situation and determine our action.

As Christians, we must bear in mind that for some of us, the anger and negative emotions we may experience due to extreme forms of abuse may take a very long time to work through and to heal. We should lose heart, however, since the Lord is with us in every step we take.

At the same time, we must emphasize that we are not meant to face certain abusive situations without the help of others. There are many forms of abuse and neglect which place great strain on our spiritual and emotional reserves. In such difficult situations, it is equally an act of wisdom and an expression of our faith to seek the assistance of caring and qualified persons. They can offer us the extra support and insight required to respond therapeutically to physical, sexual or emotional abuse.

The Blessing of the Kingdom

Our Lord declares in the final Beatitude that those who are persecuted for righteousness' sake shall possess the Kingdom of heaven.

Already in our discussion of the first Beatitude, we spoke about the significance of the term kingdom in the teachings of Jesus. It is a central theme which is expressed in both the words and the deeds of the Lord. Especially in his parables, Jesus frequently spoke about the reality of the Kingdom which signifies God's saving reign. His acts of healing and the casting out of demons bore witness to the presence of the Kingdom. Christ declared that the Kingdom was within us and he also directed his followers to pray for the coming of the Kingdom.

The phrases "Kingdom of heaven" or "Kingdom of God" are used to express the sovereign reign of God. The word Kingdom is used not primarily to describe a particular place, although a particular place may reflect God's rule. Much more deeply, the term kingdom is used to describe the sanctifying presence, the ultimate authority, and the supreme power of the Living God. He is both the source of its reality and the goal towards which all is directed. Thus, the Kingdom of God, his reign, is both present and future. It is both personal, touching the lives of each of us, and cosmic, affecting the entire creation. It is to be eagerly sought by Christ's followers. Yet, ultimately it comes as a gift. Its presence can be recognized by some but not by others. Indeed, the phrase Kingdom of God ultimately expresses God's intent to be a the center of our lives and to accept us into a relationship of love.

The coming of Christ was the decisive act of God through which he expressed his unconditional love for his creation, conquered the power of sin and death, and restored us to his fellowship. In and through Jesus Christ, the Kingdom of the

Father is made manifest by the power of the Holy Spirit. This was truly the Good News which the Lord proclaimed both through his words and through his deeds.

The reality of the Kingdom of God manifest by Christ must be received by each of us. His reign must be personally accepted by his sons and daughters. It requires, therefore, that we "repent and believe in the Good News" (Mark 1:15). God does not compel us to accept his love. He patiently waits for our free response to him. The indispensable requirement for entering into the Kingdom is that we alter the way by which we understand reality. This involves the conscious turning away from self-centeredness and the turning toward God (Mark 4:17). It necessitates that we place our trust in God and abide by his word. This involves placing the Kingdom and God's righteousness first in our lives (Matthew 6:33).

The Lord has said that it is the righteous who will shine like the sun in the Kingdom (Matthew 13:43). Trusting in the guidance of the Lord, those of us who live our lives in accordance with the Gospel will reflect the light of Christ in this world and in the age to come. United with Christ, we strive to avoid immorality and all forms of deception, and we seek to submit ourselves to the reign of God. Those of us who seek to do what is right strive to order our lives in accordance with the Gospel. We have come to know, therefore, that the Kingdom of God is one of righteousness, peace, and joy in the Holy Spirit (Romans 14:17). We shall be happy in the Lord.

From Our Christian Heritage

Whenever the temptation to offer insult seizes you, think to yourself that you are being tested: to see whether in patience you turn to God or yield in anger to the adversary. Give time to your thoughts to choose the better part. Let you either do a kindness to your enemy by an example of calmness, or defend yourself more strongly by taking no notice of him. For what is more bitter to one hostile to you than to see you indifferent to his insults? Do not leave yourself open to whoever insults you. Let him bark away. Let him explode against himself... What does it matter what name others call you? Someone shouts at you. Let you be magnanimous. Another is angry at you. Let you be gentle and mild. He will regret his words. You, however, will never regret your own practice of virtue.

St. Basil the Great[4]

Prayer

O Lover of mankind! What songs of praise, what thanks can we give to you in return for the freedom you have bestowed on us when our sins had already condemned us to death! How can we repay you for allowing us to share in the heavenly delights of the body and blood of your Christ! We entreat you: Keep us your servants and ministers, free from all condemnation. Maintain us and those present with us in honor and piety. Deem us worthy of sharing in the mysteries of your altar to our very last breath, that, having observed your commandments and attained holiness of body and soul, we may be found worthy of your heavenly kingdom, together with all who have pleased you: By the prayers and intercession of the all-holy Theotokos and all your saints.

For you are holy and full of love for us, O God, and we give you glory, Father, Son, and Holy Spirit: now and forever, and unto ages of ages. Amen.

Epilogue

The Presence of the Risen Lord

The crucifixion of the Lord may have appeared at first to many as a brutal defeat for Christ. He died a painful death surrounded for the most part by people who had come to despise him. Of his disciples, only John joined Mary, the Mother of our Lord, near the cross. A number of other women who were his followers were also close by. The other disciples had fled the scene fearing that they too might be arrested and put to death. In their moment of sorrow and fear, they seem to have forgotten that the Lord had predicted on three occasions that he would be put to death and that he would rise from the dead (Mark 8:31-33; 9:30-32; 10:32-34).

Following the death of the Lord, Joseph of Arimathea, a secret disciple who was wealthy and a member of the Sanhedrin, gathered up the courage to go to Pilate in order to request permission to bury the body of Christ. When the request was granted, Joseph arranged to have the body placed in a new tomb. As was the custom, a large stone was rolled in front of the entrance of the tomb. It was guarded by soldiers who were put there by Pilate. This was done at the request of the Jewish leaders. They believed that the disciples of Christ might come at night and secretly remove the body, and then claim that the Lord had risen (Matthew 27:62-66).

When the Sabbath was ended, some women disciples went to the tomb early in the morning of the first day of the week, which we know as the Lord's Day or Sunday. Following the custom, their purpose was to anoint the body of the Lord with spices. Because of Jewish law, this act of respect could not be done on the Sabbath. As they approached the tomb in the early hours, the earth trembled and they saw that the stone had been moved from the entrance. The guards who were posted appeared to have been knocked unconscious. Then, frightened and confused, the women encountered an angel. The messenger from God told them to look at the empty tomb and then proclaimed that Jesus had risen (Mark 16:1-8).

As the women rushed from the graveyard and headed back toward Jerusalem, they encountered the Risen Christ. When the women saw the Lord, they fell down before him expressing their awe and devotion. At that point the Lord spoke to them saying: "Do not be afraid. Go and tell my brethren to go to Galilee and they will see me" (Matthew 28:10). Overwhelmed at the Theophany which they just experienced, the women rose at once and followed the Lord's directions. They returned to the city. There, they were the first to proclaim the Resurrection of the Lord to the other disciples (Luke 24:9).

This appearance of the Risen Lord was the first of many which would occur in a period of forty days which culminated with his Ascension. At least thirteen separate appearances are recorded in the New Testament and we can safely assume that there were others which are not recorded. Each of these appearances was a distinct Theophany through which disclosed that the Lord had truly risen from the dead. As the descriptions show us, the Risen Lord was not a phantom or a ghost. He was recognizable to those present although his body was in a state of glorification.

During the period of forty days, the Lord strengthened the faith of the disciples and prepared them for their ministry. The

New Testament tells us of the Lord teaching the disciples about the meaning of the divine plan of salvation and of the significance of the Old Testament prophesies which were fulfilled by his death and resurrection. The Lord "opened their minds to understand the Scriptures..." (Luke 24:46). He also gave them instructions regarding the ministry which was ahead of them (John 20:21-23).

According to the Gospel of Saint Matthew, the final instructions which the Lord gave the disciples took place on the Mount of Olives just prior to the Ascension of Christ. The visible ministry of the Lord was completed. He was now ready to return to the glory of his Father in heaven. But before this, the Lord said to the disciples: "Go, therefore, and make disciples of all nations baptizing them in the name of the Father, and of the Son, and of the Holy Spirit, and teaching them to obey everything that I have commanded you. And remember, I am with you always, to the close of the age" (Matthew 28:20).

The disciples followed the command of the Lord. After the descent of the Holy Spirit on Pentecost, the fiftieth day after the Resurrection, they began their mission. Empowered by the Holy Spirit, they set out on missionary journeys beyond Palestine. Wherever they went, the disciples preached the Gospel. They received new members into the Church through Baptism. They led the celebration of the Eucharist. They appointed others to succeed them as the leaders of these new communities of faith and to assist them in the ministry.

The disciples knew that the message of the Gospel was meant to be a universal one. It was not to be confined only to the Jewish people of Palestine. The Gospel was meant to be preached to all peoples. The Lord had revealed the Good News about God and our relationship to him. This message of salvation was meant to be proclaimed everywhere. It was to be taught to all people.

The disciples knew that they were called by the Lord to be the instruments through which he would continue to act. They believed that the Lord had risen from the dead as he said he would. They had come to experience his presence with him long after his Ascension. The knew that he was constantly with them through the Spirit. So, they believed that the same Christ who had called them to be his followers not only directed them to go into the world as the bearers of his Gospel but also abided with them as their Lord. Although he had physically departed from their midst, the Risen Lord was not separated from His followers. He was their constant companion. The Lord was truly with them as he said he would be.

Sent by the Lord

We have frequently spoken about the call to discipleship in our discussion of the Beatitudes. The Lord has called each of us to be his follower. He calls us to abandon all attachment to evil and to orient our life toward God, our heavenly Father. Christ calls us to learn from him and to take up our cross daily and follow him (Matthew 16:24). Gifted with the presence of the Holy Spirit, we are enabled to live our lives as sons and daughters of God.

Discipleship also involves a sending. The Risen Lord sends us into the world. The same Lord who has called us to be his follower also sends us out as his ambassadors. The Good News of salvation which we have received from him is meant to be shared with others. The Lord has come for the salvation of the entire world and he has entrusted his followers with the mission of proclaiming this throughout the entire world. We cannot be followers of Christ unless we also are the messengers of his Gospel. The one who faithfully follows the Risen Lord is also one who is a missionary.

Saint John Chrysostom speaks of the responsibility of every Christian in the society when he says:

> For as the leaven converts the large quantity of meal into its own quality (Matthew 13:33), so also shall you convert the whole world... Let nobody reprove us, therefore, for being few. The power of the Gospel is great and one which once leavened becomes leaven in turn for the remainder... If twelve men leavened the whole world, imagine the extent of our weakness in that we cannot, in spite of our numbers, improve what is left. We who ought to be enough for ten thousand worlds and to become leaven to them. 'But,' you object, 'they were apostles.' So what! Were they not partakers with you? Were they not raised in cities? Did they not enjoy the same benefits?[1]

The Lord uses two very valuable images when he speaks about our responsibility as his disciples in the world. First, the Lord says to each of his followers: "You are the salt of the earth; but if salt has lost its taste, how shall its saltiness be restored? It is no longer good for anything, but is thrown out and trampled under foot" (Matthew 5:13).

Salt was frequently used as a preservative in ancient times. It prevented spoilage of perishable food in the days prior to refrigeration. It was, therefore, a very valuable and necessary commodity.

As one who is the "salt of the earth," the follower of the Lord is one who seeks to preserve those values which support and enhance the dignity of human life in accordance with the will of God. The follower of the Lord, is one who seeks to preserve what is truly good and wholesome. This is done by living our life in accordance with the Gospel, and by bearing witness in word and deed to the values of the Kingdom. As disciples of the Lord, we have a responsibility to see that human life is always treasured and to work so that the values which enhance human life are affirmed.

> The Lord also says to each of us: "You are the light of the world. A city built on a hill can not be hid. No one after lighting a lamp puts it under a bushel basket, but on the lamp stand, and it gives light to all in the house. In the same way, let your light shine before others, so that they may see your good works and give glory to your Father in heaven" (Matthew 5:14-16).

Today, as during the time of the earthly ministry of the Lord, light is necessary for our existence. Without the benefit of light, we cannot see. Darkness hides many potential dangers. With the benefit of light, however, we are able to find our way. Light enables us to see where we are going. It reveals and illuminates and warms. It allows us to avoid dangers.

As one who is the "light of the world," the follower of the Lord is a person who reflects the light of Christ. The Lord Jesus Christ is truly the light of the world (John 8:12). The disciple of the Lord not only is guided by the light of Christ but also desires to offer the light of Christ to others as they seek to better understand God, other persons, themselves, and the world. As disciples of the Lord, we have a responsibility, therefore, not to keep the light of Christ to ourselves. We cannot hide it from others! Rather, as persons who have accepted Christ as our light, we have the responsibility to assist others in receiving the light of Christ. In so doing, we let our light shine so that when others see the good which we do in the name of Christ, they will give glory to our Father in heaven.

We live in a society in which the tendency toward depersonalization is very powerful. The true dignity and inherent value of the human person are not always affirmed. Persons are frequently "valued" in our society primarily because of their economic status, their occupation, and their social achievements. Children, the elderly, the disadvantaged, the needy, the sick, the homeless, and those with disabilities are frequently not treated with the dignity they deserve as human persons. Sadly, those who are not financially wealthy or who do not appear to be successful are judged by some to be "worthless."

The Christian faith affirms a perception of the human person which is very different. As we have seen in our study of the Beatitudes, the Christian faith affirms that each person is unique and valuable. Since each of us is created in the "image and likeness" of God, none of us dispensable. Each of us is a unique person blessed by God with particular talents and abilities. We have an inherent value which is not dependent upon our age, gender, physical ability, economic statue, social achievements or our occupation. Since we belong to God, each of us is inherently valuable because of who we are, not because of what we do.

This means that our sense of "who" we are before God always has a preeminence which is meant to be expressed in our human activities. When we understand ourselves to be the daughters and sons of God first, then we are in a position to live our rives as the "light of the world" and the "salt of the earth" according to the example of the Lord. United to Christ, our light and our life, each of us has the opportunity to contribute to the well-being of others, and to affect the course of human progress through our relationships with others and our responsibilities in our home, at work, and in the society.

Saint Gregory of Nyssa emphasizes the importance of living a Christian life in the present and where we live when he says:

> Change of place does not affect any closer attachment to God. Irrespective of where you are, God will come to you if the rooms of your soul are found suitable for his occupation. But if you keep your interior full of wicked thoughts, even if you were on Golgotha, or on the Mount of Olives, even if you stood on the memorial rock of the Resurrection, you will be as removed from receiving Christ into your interior as one who has not even started to acknowledge him.[2]

When we live our lives according to the Gospel, each of us brings to our relationships a unique presence which reflects the reality of God in our life. Few days go by that we do not have contact with another person. In each of these encounters with another, we have the opportunity to meet that person truly as a person who has an inherent dignity and worth. As followers of Christ, we have the opportunity to encounter the other always in a humane and loving manner. We have the opportunity to see Christ in the other person. We also have the opportunity to present the Risen Christ to the other.

Each of us can also bring to our responsibilities a commitment which is centered upon Christ and his teachings. While many of the tasks which we are called to perform in life may appear to be similar and are often routine, each of us has the opportunity to undertake these tasks in a manner which reflects our own relationship with God.

This means that we not only can undertake our tasks in an honest and conscientious manner. It also means that we can be workers who undertake our tasks in a manner which always acknowledges the presence of God and respects the value of human life. When our tasks in the home and in the society are undertaken in the spirit of the Gospel, each of us has the unique opportunity to contribute to the proclamation of the message of Christ and the manifestation of the Kingdom in the midst of this world.

Finally, we need to remember also that our movement toward God and others in this life takes place within the physical world. For those of us who believe that the creation is fashioned by God, we know that it is within this same creation that God reveals his power and his love. The creation is not divine. It is not an end in itself. Rather, the physical world points to God its creator, redeemer, and sanctifier. Because of this, the importance of the physical creation is not to be underestimated. For those who live within this physical world with the eyes of faith, the physical is not opposed to the spiritual. Rather, it is the place in which the glory of the living God is manifest.

The creation comes to us as a gift. Every aspect of the creation is a blessing meant to inspire our love for the Father and draw us more closely to him, the creator of heaven and earth. At the same time, the creation is meant to draw us more closely to all who share this creation. The creation is meant to be a means of communion between ourselves and God as well as a means of communion among ourselves. The creation, therefore, is a common blessing which must be both respected and shared, because it is shared by God with us.

Our salvation in this life takes place within the context of the creation. Growth in holiness does not draw us away from the creation. The physical world is not by nature an obstacle to our growth toward God and others. Remembering the fact of the Incarnation of the Son of God, we need to recognize that it is in the midst of this creation that we are called by Christ to be his followers.

An ancient Christian prayer speaks about the intimate relationship which is meant to exist between Christ and his follower with these words:

> Christ be in my head and in my understanding,
> Christ be in my eyes and in my looking,
> Christ be in my mouth and in my speaking,
> Christ be in my heart and in my thinking,
> Christ be at my end and at my departing.

Throughout our discussion of the Beatitudes, we have seen that they provide us with perspectives on the manner in which we are called to live as followers of Christ in the present, as the saints of every age and place have done. Our life as disciples of the Risen Lord is meant to be distinctive. It is meant to reflect the reality of Christ and his teachings. The Beatitudes summarize the most important characteristics of our relationship with God.

The Beatitudes also provide us with guidance with regard to our relationship with others. As we have said time and again in the proceeding chapters, Christians are called to center all of our relationships and responsibilities upon Christ and his Gospel. If we take seriously our relationship with the Lord, there is no aspect of our life as Christians which can be beyond the light of Christ. Our relationship with God is intimately related to our relationship with others. Our movement toward God does not draw us away from others. On the contrary, our movement toward God always makes us more sensitive to the needs and concerns of others.

God desires that we be happy. He loves us and has created us to share in his goodness. Yet, we must choose to become sharers in joy of his Kingdom. While he loves us with a love which is unconditional, our heavenly Father always respects our freedom. He forces nothing upon us. Rather, he calls us to choose his Kingdom, to experience his love, to know his joy.

Each of the Beatitudes provides us with insight into the manner in which we can experience the "happiness" or ineffable joy which is the fruit of friendship with God. Each of the Beatitudes provides us with direction for living our life in a manner which is fully human and, at the same time, in a manner which gives glory to God now and forever and unto the ages of ages. Amen.

From Our Christian Heritage

So the Christian directs every action, small or great, according to the will of God, performing the action at the same time with care and exactitude, and keeping his thoughts fixed upon the One who gave him the work to do. In this way, he fulfills the sayings, "I set the Lord always in my sight; for he is at my right hand, that I be not moved" and he observes the precept, "Whether you eat or drink or whatever else you do, do all to the glory of God." We should perform every action as if under the eye of the Lord and think every thought as if observed by him... fulfilling the words of the Lord: "I seek not my own will but the will of him who sent me, the Father."

St. Basil the Great[3]

Prayer

By the genius of your wisdom, O Lord, our Lord, the day attains its length, the powers of heaven praise you, and every living being is drawn to worship you according to its own capacity. We beseech you: Give us the grace of a peaceful day, so that we may live in a way that is pleasing to you and pure, maintaining our hearts free of every stain at all times, while enjoying the benefits of your gifts to the full. And count us ever more worthy of blessing your generosity and goodness without fear of condemnation.

For you deserve all glory, honor, and worship, Father, Son, and Holy Spirit: now and forever and unto ages of ages. Amen.

Notes

Introduction
1. St. Augustine, *Sermon on the Beatitudes*

Chapter 1 - Blessed are the poor in spirit
1. St. Gregory of Narek, *The Lamentations*
2. St. John Chrysostom, *Homily on the Statues*, 2:15
3. St. Basil, *Homily on Fasting*.
4. St. John Chrysostom, *Homily on Almsgiving*, 50
5. St. Basil, *Homily on Humility*, 20

Chapter 2 - Blessed are those who mourn
1. St. John Climacus, *The Ladder*, Step 5
2. St. John of Kronstadt, *My Life in Christ*, 12
3. St. John Chrysostom, *Homily on Matthew*, 15
4. Ibid, 24
5. St. John Chrysostom, *Homily on Acts of the Apostles*, 20.4
6. St. Julian of Norwich, *Revelations of Divine Love*, 56

Chapter 3 - Blessed are the meek
1. St. Basil, *Ascetical Principles*, 1
2. St. Nicholas Cabasilas, *On the Divine Liturgy*, 2:132
3. St. Basil, *Homily on the Love of God and Neighbor*, 3
4. Dorotheus of Gaza, *Instructions*, 6
5. St. Gregory of Nyssa, *On the Song of Songs*, 2
6. St. Macarius of Egypt, *Fifty Spiritual Homilies*
7. St. Macrina, cited in Gregory of Nyssa, *The Soul and Resurrection*, 8

Chapter 4 - Blessed are those who hunger and thirst
1. St Augustine, *The Confessions*, 1.1
2. St. John Chrysostom, *Homily on the Gospel of John*, 10
3. St. Gregory of Nyssa, *On the Song of Songs*, Homily 8
4. St.Ambrose of Milan, *On Virginity*, 16:99
5. St. Leo of Rome, *Sermon on the Beatitudes*
6. St. Cyprian of Carthage, *Letter to Donatus*.

Chapter 5 - Blessed are the merciful
1. St. Peter Chrysologus, *Sermon 148*
2. St. John Chrysostom, *Second Address on Baptism*
3. Apophthegmata, *St. Antony the Great*, 9
4. St. Gregory of Nyssa, *On the Beatitudes*, Homily 5
5. St. Isaac the Syrian, *Concerning the Distinction of Virtues*, 91
6. St. Gregory the Theologian, *Homily on the Love of the Poor,* 16

Chapter 6 - Blessed are the pure in heart
1. St. Gregory of Nyssa, *On the Song of Songs*, Homily 2
2. Attributed to St. Basil the Great
3. St. John Chrysostom, *Homily on Genesis* 2.1
4. St. Pachomius, *Life of St. Pachomius*
5. St. Gregory of Nyssa, *On the Beatitudes,* Homily 6
6. St. Gregory of Nyssa, *The Life of Moses*

Chapter 7 - Blessed are the peacemakers
1. St. Nicholas Cabasilas, *The Life in Christ*, 1.1
2. St. Gregory of Nyssa, *On the Beatitudes*, Homily 7
3. Ibid.
4. St. Maximos the Confessor, *Centuries on Charity*

Biographical Notes

Throughout this study we quoted a number of Fathers and Mothers of the Church. We thought it would be helpful to introduce each of them with a biographical note.

St. Ambrose of Milan, c. 339-977, was born in the old Roman city of Augusta Treverorum, the modern Trier. As a young man, he studied law and rhetoric in Rome. Following his father's example, he chose to be a civil servant and subsequently became a governor in the region of Milan. While still a catechumen, he was known for his faith and his concern for reconciliation among divided Christians. Because of this, he was elected the Bishop of Milan by the acclamation of the people in 374. Following his baptism and ordination, he came to be regarded as a champion of the poor as well as a thoughtful teacher, preacher, and writer. His *Homily on Virginity* extols the characteristics of purity of life. His better known work is *On the Sacraments*. His Feastday is December 7.

St. Anthony the Great, c. 251-356, was born near the city of Memphis in Egypt. As a young man, he was inspired to give away his belongings and to enter the monastic life under the direction of an elder. After some time, he went into the desert where he lived as a hermit for about twenty years. However, his reputation for piety and charity soon attracted many who sought his guidance. He had a powerful impact upon the lives of many and was regarded as one of the pioneers of Christian monasticism. A small number of *Letters* of St. Anthony have survived. St. Athanasius wrote *The Life of St. Anthony* not long after his death. His Feastday is January 17.

St. Augustine of Hippo, 354-430, is regarded as one of the most influential theologians of early Western Christianity. Born at Thagaste in Numidia, present day Algeria, Augustine later studied philosophy and rhetoric in Carthage. While his mother, Monica, was a Christian, Augustine initially repudiated the faith and lived the life of a prodigal. While in Milan, he later came under the influence of St. Ambrose. After much personal struggle described in his autobiography, *Confessions*, Augustine became a Christian in 386. Returning to North Africa, Augustine was ordained a priest and after some time the Bishop of Hippo in 396 at the request of the people. A remarkable teacher and writer, he opposed a number of heresies and sectarian movements in North Africa. Among his many writings are his autobiography *The Confessions, The City of God*, and *On the Trinity*. His Feastday is August 28 in the Western churches and June 14 in the Orthodox Church.

St. Basil the Great, c. 329-379, came from a very pious and affluent family in Caesarea in Cappadocia, present day Asia Minor. The church honors as saints his grandmother, mother, father, sister and two brothers. His early studies in Constantinople and Athens prepared him to be a teacher of rhetoric. However, under the influence of his sister, St. Macrina, Basil was directed towards the monastic life which he experienced in Syria, Mesopotamia and Syria. Upon his return home, Basil eventually established a monastic community near Neo-Caesarea in Pontos, near the Black Sea. With the guidance of St. Macrina, Basil established a Rule for the community which has greatly influenced monasticism. At the request of the local bishop, Basil was ordained a priest and later became a Bishop of Caesarea in 370. He served the church with remarkable wisdom and devotion. A champion of the poor and oppressed, he established a small city, known as the "Basileias" to care for those in need. Together with his brother, St. Gregory of Nyssa, and his friend, St. Gregory the Theologian, Basil helped the church to articulate its faith in the face of the Arian heresy which denied the full divinity of Christ. In addition to this, prayers, which he composed continue to be used in a Liturgy bearing his name in the Orthodox Church. Honored as a person of prayer, charity and wisdom, Basil was mourned by Christians, Jews and Pagans when he died in 379. Among his many writings, are his *Homilies, Letters* and On *the Holy Spirit*, as well as the *Long Rules* and the *Short Rules*. His Feastday is January 1 in the Orthodox Church and January 2 in many Western churches.

St. Cyprian, c. 200-258, was born and raised in Carthage, North Africa. Having studied philosophy and rhetoric, he subsequently became an advocate in the civil courts before his conversion to Christianity about 245. Within a few years, he was ordained a priest and in 248 was elected the Bishop of Carthage. Living at a time when Christians were actively persecuted by the pagan Roman government, Cyprian was ready to receive back into the Church those who had abandoned their faith during persecutions but later repented. Because of this, the Donatists opposed him, a heretical group who refused to receive those Christians who had apostatized during persecutions. During the persecutions of Emperor Valerian, Cyprian was exiled in 257 and put to death in 258. Among his writings, the *Letter to Donatus* speaks of Cyprian's journey from Paganism to Christianity. His Feastday is October 2.

St. Dorotheus of Gaza, c. 506-560, was raised in a cultured and affluent Christian family in Antioch, Syria. Before departing for the monastery in Gaza, Dorotheus undoubtedly enjoyed the benefits of a classical education. In the monastery, he became a spiritual son to the renowned elders Barsanuphius and John. After their death, Dorotheus left Gaza about 540 and established his own monastic community. There he became an elder to a community of monastics. His famous *Instructions* were initially the practical guidance which he offered to the community. His vision of the monastery not only emphasized the particular responsibilities of each member but also stressed the value of community life. His insights and council have had a profound impact upon Eastern Christian monasticism. His Feastday is June 5.

St. Francis of Assisi, 1181-1226, was the son of a wealthy merchant in the city of Assisi in Umbria, Italy. As a young man, Francis worked with his father in his cloth business and was an important member of the local community. While on a military expedition, Francis had a dream in which Christ called him to serve the poor. He later had another experience in which he was directed to rebuild a run down church building. This and other experiences led him to choose the life of a hermit and devote himself to caring for the needy especially for the lepers. After a few years, a number of disciples gathered about Francis. They established small and very simple monastic community near Assisi. Using this as a base, they set out to preach to the poor in the region. Francis reacted against the affluent and privileged life of many of the existing monastic communities in Western Europe. He called for a return to the simple values of the Gospel. These concerns are expressed in his *Prayer*, his *Canticle of the Son* and in his *Testament*. While Francis was against the establishment of a highly structured monastic community, the Church of Rome approved his simple monastic rule in 1210. A few years later, Francis encouraged Clare of Assisi to establish a similar monastic community for women. His Feastday is October 4.

St. Gregory of Narek, c. 945-1003, is associated with the small town of his birth located on the southern side of Lake Van in the region of greater Armenia. Gregory was raised in a deeply religious family. His father and two older brother were priests. Gregory entered the local monastery as a young man and devoted himself both to monastic discipline and to learning. As time went on, he gained a reputation of being not only a outstanding student of theology but also a keen observer of nature. He often spent time in meditation along the shore of Lake Van. He wrote a number of letters and hymns. At about the age of fifty, Gregory was inspired to write about his insights in the form of a Prayer Book, usually known as the *Lamentations*, containing ninety-five chapters. His Feastday is October 14.

St. Gregory of Nyssa, c. 335-395, was the younger brother of both St. Basil and St. Macrina. Like his brother, Gregory received an outstanding education in Athens and was also greatly influenced by his sister. He later married Theosevia, a women known also for her faith and education. Intending to be a teacher, Gregory was encouraged by Basil and Gregory the Theologian to enter the active service of the ministry of the Church. He was ordained the Bishop of Nyssa, a remote outpost near Armenia, in 371. Also honored as a saint, Theosevia was ordained a deacon. Five years later, however, a rival party following the teaching of Arius which denied the full divinity of Christ deposed Gregory. He was subsequently restored to his see by the acclamation of the people. Together with those of Basil and Gregory the Theologian, Gregory's sermons and writings contributed to the reconciliation of most of the Arians by the time of the Council of Constantinople in 381. A prolific writer, Gregory frequently wrote to explicate the faith of the Church in opposition to distorted teachings. In addition to such works as *The Great Catechism*, Gregory also devoted much thought to exegeting scriptural themes. Among these are his eight homilies *On the Beatitudes*. His Feastday is January 10 in the Orthodox Church and March 9 in many Western Churches.

St. Gregory the Theologian, c. 330-390, was raised in a deeply pious and affluent family in the region of Cappadocia, Gregory was the son of the bishop of Nazianzus with whom he shared the same first name. Educated in Caesarea and Alexandria, Gregory also studied in Athens where Basil and he developed a lifelong friendship. Ordained a priest by his father, Gregory sought a simple ministry which emphasized the care for the poor. At the insistence of Basil, however, Gregory was called to be bishop of the small town of Sasima. Like Basil, he also became a thoughtful exponent of the faith of the Church at a time of great divisions among Christians over the proper understanding of the person of Christ and of the Holy Spirit. Gregory's sermons reflected not only his deep faith in the Trinity but also his concern for the needy. He participated in the Council of Constantinople in 381 and was elected Patriarch in the same year. Not long thereafter, he retired and returned to a monastic style of life at his family's home in Arianzus. While best known for his *Theological Orations*, Gregory's *Homily on the Poor* reflect both his powerful preaching ability and his concern for the less fortunate. His Feastday is January 25 in the Orthodox Church and January 2 in many Western Churches.

St. Isaac the Syrian of Nineveh (seventh century) was born at Berth-Katrage on the shores of the Persian Gulf in the region of modern Qatar. While little is known of his early life, he was a monk who was elected the bishop of Nineveh about 660. This see was part of the Church of the Persian Empire. After serving for a short time, he retired to the mountains and eventually settled in the monastery of Rabdan Shabbur. Perhaps while serving as the spiritual father, his teaching were gathered into what are now called the *Ascetic Treatises*. His Feastday is January 28.

St. Innocent of Alaska, 1797-1879, came to Russian Alaska as a missionary in 1824. An earlier group of Orthodox missionaries had begun their work in 1794 shortly after the discovery of Alaska by Russian explorers. Then known as Fr. John Veniaminov, he was among the most active of missionaries to serve in Alaska. In order to aid his missionary work among the Aleuts on Unalaska, Innocent created an alphabet based upon Cyrillic characters. A dictionary and grammar soon followed. This provided the basis for the translation of the Gospel of St. Matthew and portions of the Liturgy into the Aleut language. He also wrote a basic catechism, *Indication of the Pathway into the Kingdom of Heaven*. Concerned with the total welfare of the natives, Innocent also taught them agricultural skills, carpentry, and metalworking. He constructed a school and orphanage as well as a number of chapels. After ten years, he and his family moved to Sitka where he continued his missionary work. Following the death of his wife, he became a monk and received the name Innocent. He was soon elected the bishop of the diocese which included Alaska and Eastern Siberia in 1840. Deeply committed to missionary work, he was subsequently elected Archbishop of Yakutsk in Eastern Siberia in 1852 and later Metropolitan of Moscow in 1858. He was proclaimed a saint in 1977. His Feastday is March 31.

St. John Cassian, c. 360-433, spent time as a young monk in monastic communities both in Bethlehem and in Egypt. Ordained a deacon by St. John Chrysostom, he remained a close assistant to the Patriarch of Constantinople for some years. When Chrysostom was deposed under imperial pressure, John Cassian carried his appeal to Pope Innocent I in Rome in 405. From that time, it appears that John Cassian spent the remainder of his life in Western Europe where he was instrumental in spreading monastic traditions of the East. Most probably ordained a priest at Marseilles, he founded separate monasteries for men and women there about 415. His *Institutes* are devoted to the principles of community life and his *Conferences* contain the homilies of Egyptian monastics as retold by him. His Feastday is February 29.

St. John Chrysostom, 354-407, was raised in Antioch, Syria in a prominent Christian family. Following his education in law and oratory, John set out to be a monk in a community not far from the city. He later returned to Antioch and was ordained a deacon in 381 and a priest in 386. While caring for the poor of the city, he was recognized also for his powerful preaching and was given the title "Chrysostom" which means the "golden-mouth." Elected the Archbishop of Constantinople in 398, he immediately championed the cause of the poor, and challenged the low morality of many clergy and members of the imperial family. Falsely charged by opponents in the church and government, John was deposed as Patriarch and briefly exiled. Returning to the capital city, John continued to criticize the immorality and abuses of both church leaders and members of the imperial family. A second exile began in 404 when he was sent to Armenia. Through visits from friends and through letters to the deaconess Olympia, the influence of John continued unabated. Again, the government intervened and ordered him deported to the shores of the Black Sea. During the difficult journey, John died in 407 at Comna in Pontos. John is regarded as one of the most insightful exegete of the Scriptures. Several of his extensive *Homilies* on biblical books are preserved. He also contributed many of the prayers to the "Liturgy of St. John Chrysostom" still in use in the Orthodox Church. His Feastday is November 13 in the Orthodox Church and September 13 in many Western Churches.

St. John Climacus (of the Ladder), c. 524-600, entered the monastery of Mount Sinai at the age of sixteen and came under the direction of an elder whose name was Abba Martyrios. Tonsured a monk four years later, John remained in the monastery for about twenty years before he set out to live as a hermit in a nearby cell. His reputation soon spread and he was visited by countless other monks seeking his advice. At the age of seventy-five, John was elected as the abbot of the Monastery of Mount Sinai. It was during this period of time that he composed his classic work, the *Ladder of Divine Assent*, at the request of a neighboring abbot. Written primarily for monks, the *Ladder* is composed of thirty short chapters subsequently called steps. Dealing with both virtues and vices, the Ladder is a compilation of early Christian monastic insights coming from the first three centuries of the Church and reflecting the culture of that time. His Feastdays are March 30 and the Fourth Sunday of Great Lent.

St. John Sergieff of Kronstadt, 1829-1908, was born in Soura in the region of Arkhangelsk in Northern Russia. Coming from a poor family, his parents nurtured him in the faith and sought to provide him with a basic education. As a young man, he entered the famous Theological Academy of St. Petersburg. During his studies, he thought of becoming a monk and a missionary to Siberia. However, in time he was drawn to the ministry of preaching the faith to those who were only nominal Christians. Following his marriage, John was ordained a priest. He and his wife moved to Kronstadt, a port city not far from St. Petersburg. There, Fr. John was assigned to the Cathedral. He remained in this parish for 51 years. During this time, he was recognized for his piety, his charity and his wise counsel. He centered his daily life upon regular prayer and the Eucharist. He became known for his care for the poor, the sick and the needy children of the city. Countless people sought his pastoral direction. Fr. John's famous book, *My Life in Christ*, is actually a diary containing reflections on the nature of the Christian life. His Feastday is December 20.

St. Julian of Norwich, c. 1342-1416, was a monastic who lived for about forty years at the church of St. Julian in Norwich, England. Julian came to be highly esteemed because of her profound spiritual experiences which bear witness to the infinite love of God. Her insights were committed to writing in 1373. About twenty years later in 1393, she again wrote about the experience and provided some further reflections. Her writings were titled *Revelations of Divine Love*. Her Feastday is May 8.

St. Leo of Rome, d. 461, was probably born in Rome in the late fourth century. While nothing is known of his youth, he served with great distinction as a deacon to a number of bishops in Rome. Leo was elected the Bishop of Rome in 440. For about twenty years, Pope Leo guided the Church of Rome at a crucial period. Highly regarded for his theological insights, he was a staunch defender of the faith of the Church in the face of a number of heresies. His classic statement on Christology, known as the Tome of Leo, was read at the Council of Chalcedon in 451. He also acted to free the city Rome from the control of the Germanic tribes. Over a hundred of his *Letters* survive. His Feastday is November 10 in the Western Churches and February 18 in the Orthodox Church.

St. Macarius of Egypt, c. 300-390, was born in upper Egypt and became a monk at about the age of thirty. He is remembered as one of the great monastic teachers who lived in the Egyptian desert for over sixty years. He was a disciple of St. Anthony the Great and was, therefore, associated with the development of the earliest forms of monasticism. His *Spiritual Homilies* were most probably instructions given to the many monks who sought his guidance. His Feastday is January 19.

St. Macrina, c. 327-379, was the oldest of ten children in the pious family which included St. Basil and St. Gregory of Nyssa. While the culture of her day did not permit her to benefit from the same formal education as her brothers, Macrina is remembered for her deep faith and wisdom which had a profound impact upon them especially after the death of her fiancé. Her insights into the significance of communal monasticism guided St. Basil in the organization of his monasteries and the composition of his *Rules*. In addition, Gregory has integrated some of her perspectives on the meaning of the Resurrection into his essay *On the Soul and the Resurrection*. Not long after her death, Gregory wrote the *Life of Macrina* in which he honors his sister and discusses the remarkable features of her life and her influence. Her Feastday is July 19

St. Maximos the Confessor, 580-662, was probably orphaned at the age of nine and entrusted to the care of a monastery in Palestine. In 614, he and others fled Palestine in the face of the Persian invasion and settled in a monastery near Constantinople. After serving briefly as a secretary for Emperor Heraclius, Maximos traveled to Carthage where he continued to live as a monk. As one of the most influential theologians of his time, Maximos opposed any notion which diminished the full humanity as well as full divinity of Christ. He affirmed that Christ had a human will as well as a divine will. His appreciation of the full humanity of Christ led him to forcefully affirm the dignity of the human person, the centrality of human freedom and the goodness of creation, all seen in the light of God's love. Because of his fierce opposition to the heresy of monothelitism, which was for a time supported both by the government and by the church in Constantinople, Maximos was exiled to Thrace. Called back to the capital in 662, Maximos continued to oppose the heresy. His right hand and tongue were cut off. Exiled again, this time to the region of the Black Sea, Maximos died there. Because of his witness and teaching, the heresy of monothelitism was eventually repudiated at the Council of Constantinople in 660-661. Much of Maximos' writings are collected under the title *Centuries on Charity*. His Feastday is January 21.

St. Pachomius, 287-347, was raised in a pagan family in Upper Egypt. When he was about twenty, Pachomius joined the army. While at the city of Thebes, he enjoyed the hospitality of a Christian community. So strong was their witness of love to a pagan army recruit, Pachomius resolved to follow their example. After being discharged, he eventually received Christian instruction and was baptized. For the next seven years, an old hermit guided him in the ways of the monastic life. Eventually, a number of other men who were attracted to the monastic life sought out Pachomius as their elder. Writing in Coptic, Pachomius fashioned a *Rule* to guide the new monastic community as well as a similar one created for women. Because of his profound influence, Pachomius is often regarded as the founder of communal or cenobitic monasticism. His Feastday is November 29.

St. Peter Chrysologus, d.c. 450, was a native of the Italian city of Imola. As a young deacon, he was active in the struggle against paganism and in the development of Christian communities. He subsequently was elected the Archbishop of Ravenna and was known for his forceful preaching. Because of this, he received the title "Chrysologus" which means "golden word." Several of his *Homilies* have survived. His Feastday is July 30 in many Western Churches.